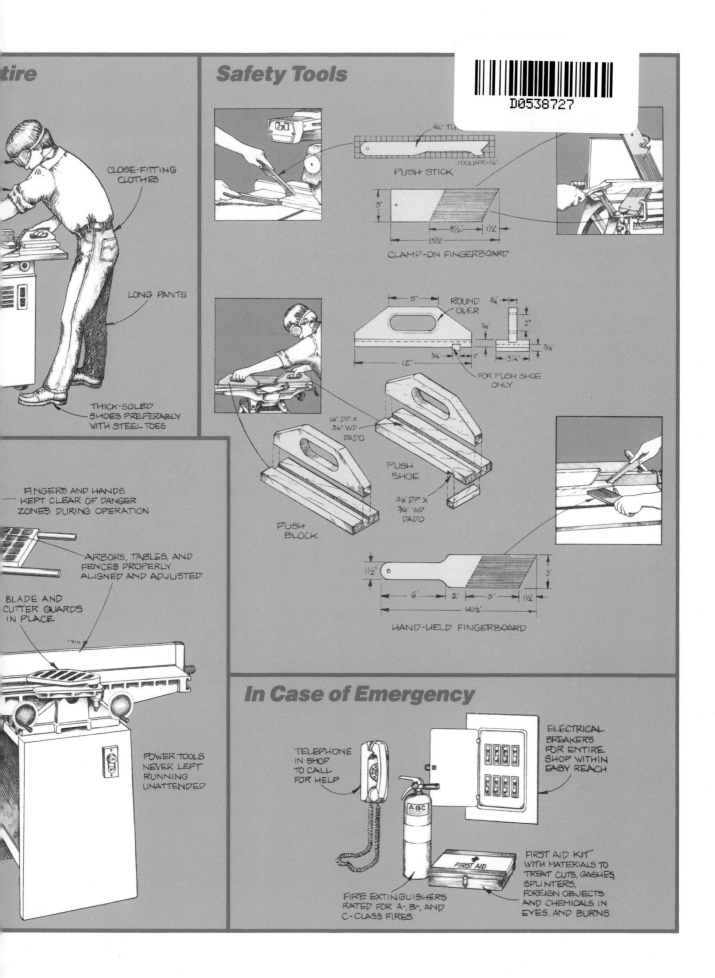

...tire

Safety Tools

CLOSE-FITTING CLOTHES

LONG PANTS

THICK-SOLED SHOES PREFERABLY WITH STEEL TOES

PUSH STICK

3/4" TH

1 SQUARE = 1/2"

CLAMP-ON FINGERBOARD

3"

8 1/2" 1 1/2"

13 1/2"

ROUND OVER

5" 3/4"

3/4"

12" 3/4" 1"

2"

3 1/4"

3/4"

FOR PUSH SHOE ONLY

FINGERS AND HANDS KEPT CLEAR OF DANGER ZONES DURING OPERATION

1/4" DP X 3/4" WD DADO

PUSH SHOE

3/8" DP X 3/4" WD DADO

PUSH BLOCK

ARBORS, TABLES, AND FENCES PROPERLY ALIGNED AND ADJUSTED

BLADE AND CUTTER GUARDS IN PLACE

1 1/2"

6" 2" 5" 1 1/2"

14 1/2"

3"

HAND-HELD FINGERBOARD

POWER TOOLS NEVER LEFT RUNNING UNATTENDED

In Case of Emergency

TELEPHONE IN SHOP TO CALL FOR HELP

ELECTRICAL BREAKERS FOR ENTIRE SHOP WITHIN EASY REACH

ABC

FIRST AID

FIRE EXTINGUISHERS RATED FOR A-, B-, AND C- CLASS FIRES

FIRST AID KIT WITH MATERIALS TO TREAT CUTS, GASHES, SPLINTERS, FOREIGN OBJECTS AND CHEMICALS IN EYES, AND BURNS.

·BUILD·IT·BETTER·YOURSELF·
WOODWORKING PROJECTS

Benches, Swings, and Gliders

Collected and Written
by Nick Engler

Rodale Press
Emmaus, Pennsylvania

If you have any questions or comments concerning this book, please write:
Rodale Press
Book Reader Service
33 East Minor Street
Emmaus, PA 18098

Series Editor: Jeff Day
Managing Editor/Author: Nick Engler
Editor: Roger Yepsen
Copy Editor: Mary Green
Graphic Designer: Linda Watts
Graphic Artists: Christine Vogel
                Chris Walendzak
Photography: Karen Callahan
Cover Photography: Mitch Mandel
Cover Photograph Stylist: Janet C. Vera
Proofreader: Hue Park
Typesetting by Computer Typography, Huber Heights, Ohio
Interior Illustrations by Mary Jane Favorite, Scot T. Marsh, and
 O'Neil & Associates, Dayton, Ohio
Endpaper Illustrations by Mary Jane Favorite
Produced by Bookworks, Inc., West Milton, Ohio

Library of Congress Cataloging-in-Publication Data

Engler, Nick.
    Benches, swings, and gliders / collected and written by Nick
Engler.
        p.   cm.—(Build-it-better-yourself woodworking
projects)
    ISBN 0–87857–943–5: hardcover
    1. Outdoor furniture.   2. Benches.   3. Swings.   I. Title.
II. Title: Gliders.   III. Series: Engler, Nick. Build-it-better-
yourself woodworking projects.
TT197.5.09E63   1991
684.1'8—dc20   90–20742
                                                CIP

6 8 10 9 7   hardcover

Contents

Sitting and Setting

Not long ago, sociologists from New York University studied New York City's parks to find out why some were popular gathering places and others were little used. At first, the scientists concentrated on the park *setting*. They examined the landscaping, the types and numbers of trees and shrubs, whether or not the parks had streams or ponds, how close the parks were to stores and restaurants. Their initial findings were confusing: Some poorly landscaped or inconveniently located parks were just as popular as other parks with beautiful, convenient settings.

The NYU sociologists made a second, more detailed survey, examining the physical equipment in the parks as well as the setting. This time, the answer was apparent. The most popular parks were the ones with the most benches and other forms of seating. In other words, *sitting* was much more important than *setting*.

There were several other interesting findings. The most popular type of park seating was *movable* seating — benches that could be picked up and rearranged. The scientists determined that people liked to group the seats so they could sit and talk. And if they had to settle for anchored seating, people preferred long benches, apparently because they could turn and face one another while they conversed. Surprisingly, comfort was of little consequence. People would sit on hard wooden benches for hours as long as they could talk to one another. Comfort took a back seat to conversation.

Swings and gliders, the scientists found, were perennial favorites, and were just as likely to be used by adults as children. Children were apt to play on them, but adults sat and swayed and talked. The gentle motion relaxed the older folks and put them at ease. This, in turn, seemed to stimulate conversation.

Although this study concerned large urban parks, the conclusions have a direct bearing on your home. As you landscape your property, don't just focus on the plants — where to put the trees and shrubs, whether to plant annual or perennial flowers. Consider the *people* who will visit your yard. How will you accommodate them and help them to enjoy one another's company? Where, amongst the foliage, will they sit?

Try thinking of your yard as if it were another room in your house. Treat the outdoor furniture as exactly that — *furniture*. Consider that the plants are just accessories and decorations. Do what you'd normally do to make a room livable — arrange the furniture first, then add the accessories and decorations. Benches, swings, and other forms of outdoor seating assume new importance in this light. They become focal points in your yard, rather than afterthoughts.

Also consider providing several different types of seating. You don't have just one kind of chair in your home; you need a variety for different functions and occasions. Your yard is no different. It helps to have a mixture of utilitarian and formal, plain and fancy.

All this isn't to say that plants aren't significant — you mustn't let the benches and swings crowd out the flowers. But while landscaping and gardening help create an agreeable setting, they are not as consequential as once thought. Of all the things you can do to make your yard a pleasant place, the most important is to provide a place to sit and enjoy it. Furthermore, you need to provide a seat for another person besides yourself — or, even better, seating for several people. A backyard is so much more enjoyable when there are friends to share it.

Victorian Porch Swing

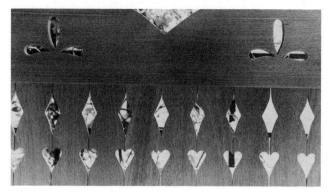

The concept of outdoor furniture began in Victorian times. Among the well-to-do English in the nineteenth century, it was fashionable to keep landscaped gardens. To better enjoy these gardens, they adapted or invented several distinct furniture forms — furniture that was meant to be left outside, providing a place to rest and reflect among the flowers and shrubs.

One of the most popular pieces of outdoor furniture was the garden swing — a settee without legs, suspended from a tree limb or frame. The design spread across the Atlantic, where Americans enjoyed their porches with the same relish that the English did their gardens. We quickly discovered that this swing could be hung from the joists of a porch roof, and the porch swing became a common sight in front of American homes.

The porch swing shown was built by Larry Callahan of West Milton, Ohio, to grace the porch of his Victorian home. Like so many built during the Victorian era, the swing is easy to make but highly decorative. The "carpenter gothic" back splats and top back rail with fretwork both add ornament to the simple, sturdy construction. ●

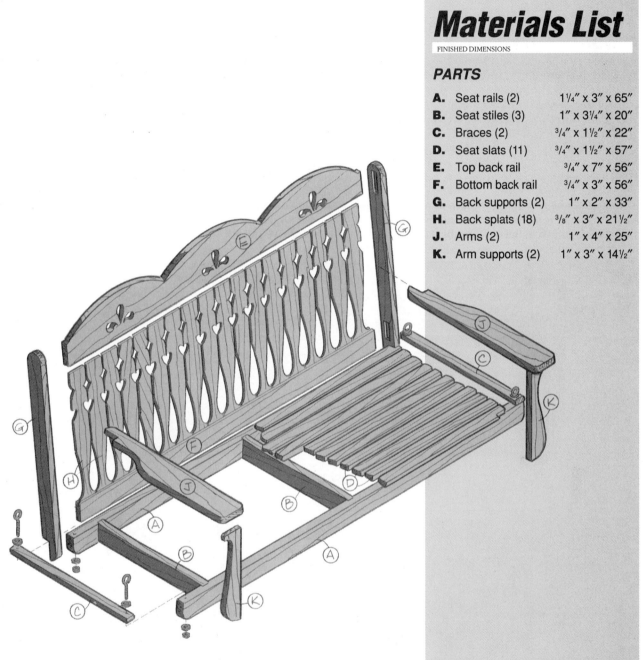

EXPLODED VIEW

Materials List

FINISHED DIMENSIONS

PARTS

A.	Seat rails (2)	1¼" x 3" x 65"
B.	Seat stiles (3)	1" x 3¼" x 20"
C.	Braces (2)	¾" x 1½" x 22"
D.	Seat slats (11)	¾" x 1½" x 57"
E.	Top back rail	¾" x 7" x 56"
F.	Bottom back rail	¾" x 3" x 56"
G.	Back supports (2)	1" x 2" x 33"
H.	Back splats (18)	⅜" x 3" x 21½"
J.	Arms (2)	1" x 4" x 25"
K.	Arm supports (2)	1" x 3" x 14½"

HARDWARE

#10 x 1½" Brass flathead wood screws (24–30)
4d Galvanized finishing nails (¼ lb.)
⅜" x 5" Eye bolts (4)
⅜" Stop nuts (4)
⅜" Flat washers (8)
Porch swing chains with 5' leaders
2" S-hooks (6)
⅜" Screw hooks (2)

1 ***Select the stock and cut the parts to size.*** To make this project, you need about 6 board feet of 8/4 (eight-quarters) stock, 8 board feet of 5/4 (five-quarters) stock, and 22 board feet of 4/4 (four-quarters) stock. The species of wood you use will depend on where you want to mount the swing. If you plan to hang the swing in a sheltered area such as a porch or gazebo, you can use almost any cabinet-grade lumber. (Oak is traditional — the swing shown is made from red oak.) If you want to hang it out in the weather, use a weather-resistant "outdoor" wood, such as

mahogany, teak, cedar, cypress, or redwood.

Avoid pressure-treated lumber. While some heavier outdoor furniture can be made from this construction-grade wood, the parts of the swing are too delicate. They may split, check, or splinter.

After selecting the wood, cut the parts to the sizes given in the Materials List. Make the seat rails from the 8/4 stock, the seat stiles, arms, arm supports, and back supports from the 5/4 stock, and the remaining parts from the 4/4 stock.

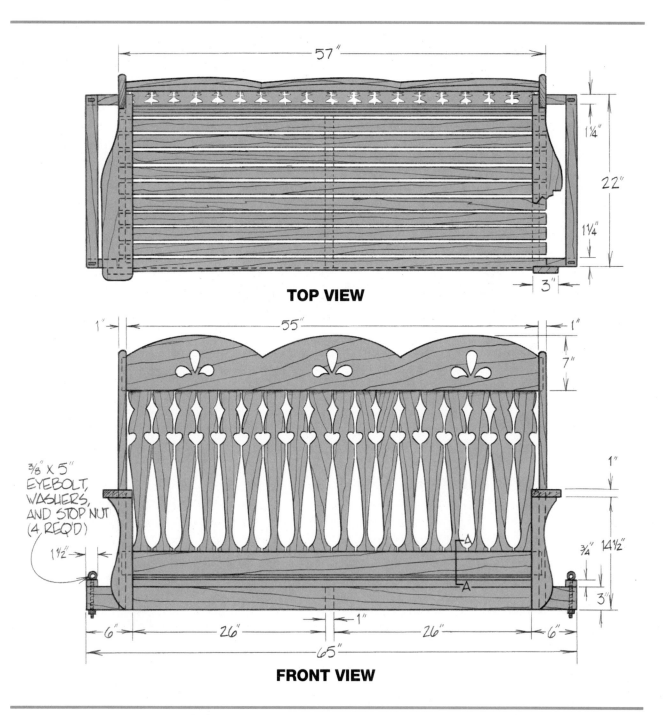

2 Cut the joints.

The swing is assembled with several simple joints — dadoes, grooves, and mortises. Here's a list:

- 1"-wide, ¼"-deep dadoes in the seat rails to hold the seat stiles, as shown in the *Seat Rail Layout*
- ¾"-wide, 4"-long, ½"-deep mortises in the back supports to hold the back rails, as shown in the *Back Support Layout*
- ⅜"-wide, ½"-deep grooves in the back rails to hold the back splats, as shown in *Section A*

Make the dadoes and grooves with either a dado cutter or a table-mounted router. The easiest tool for making the mortises is a hand-held router. After routing the mortises, square the ends with a chisel. (See Figures 1 through 3.)

1/To rout the mortises in a back support, first clamp a back support and a large scrap (1" thick and at least 4" wide) to the workbench, edge to edge. The scrap will give you the extra support you need for the router. Nail a straight, narrow scrap to the top of the larger one to guide the router.

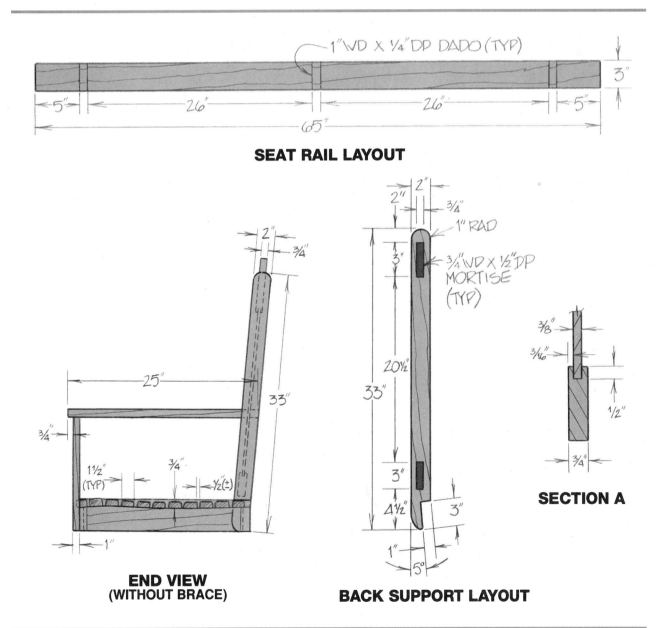

1"WD X ¼"DP DADO (TYP)

3"

5" — 26" — 26" — 5"

65"

SEAT RAIL LAYOUT

2"
¾"

25"

33"

¾"

1½" (TYP)

¾"

½"(±)

1"

END VIEW
(WITHOUT BRACE)

2"
2"
¾"
1" RAD

3"

¾"WD X ½"DP MORTISE (TYP)

20½"

33"

3"

4½"

1"

5°

BACK SUPPORT LAYOUT

⅜"
3⁄16"
½"
¾"

SECTION A

2/Rout each mortise in several passes, cutting just ⅛″ – ¼″ deeper with each pass. Remember that both ends of the mortise are blind. Stop cutting just as the bit touches the layout line at each end of the mortise.

3/Finish each mortise by squaring the ends with a chisel.

TRY THIS! To begin cutting a mortise with an ordinary hand-held router, first drill a stopped hole in the waste. This hole must be the same diameter as the bit and as deep as you want to make the mortise. Place the bit in the hole, make sure you have a firm hold on the router, and turn it on. (Initially, the bit may catch on the side of the hole and jerk the router sideways slightly. This jerk isn't hard to control, provided you have a secure grip on the router. In addition, you can greatly reduce the severity of this jerk by taking shallow bites.) If you have a plunge router, you needn't worry about drilling a starting hole — just push the bit down into the wood.

3 **Cut the parts to shape.** Many of the parts of this swing are shaped for either comfort or decoration. Since you must make at least two copies of most shapes, tape the identical parts together and cut two or more parts at once. Wipe the wood with a tack cloth first to remove the sawdust. (This will ensure that the tape adheres properly — tape doesn't stick well to a dusty surface.) Stack the boards so the edges and ends are flush, then stick them together with double-faced carpet tape.

Note: Make two or more stacks when cutting the back splats. Since there are 18 of these parts, a single stack would be too thick to cut safely.

Enlarge the *Top Back Rail Pattern* and trace it onto the stock. Also enlarge the *Arm, Arm Support, Seat Stile, and Back Splat Pattern*. Mark these shapes on the top board in each of their respective stacks. Lay out the shape of the back support on the top board of the back support stack, as shown in the *Back Support Layout*.

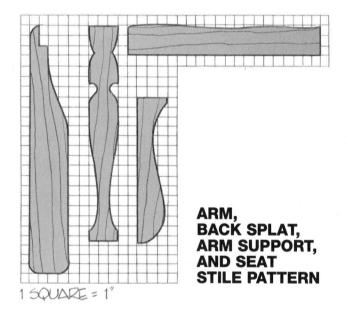

1 SQUARE = 1″

**ARM,
BACK SPLAT,
ARM SUPPORT,
AND SEAT
STILE PATTERN**

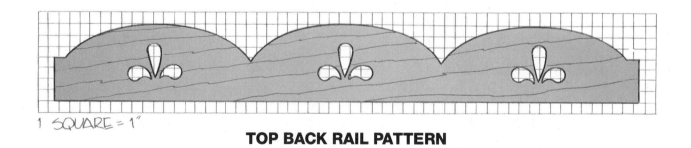

1 SQUARE = 1″

TOP BACK RAIL PATTERN

Cut all these shapes with a band saw and a saber saw. Make the outside shapes with a band saw and the inside shapes (the cutouts in the top back rail) with a saber saw. (See Figure 4.) If you use a saber saw to cut both the inside and outside shapes, remember you can only cut a stack 1½"–2" thick — you must make at least four separate stacks for the back splats. When you've sawed all the shapes, sand the sawed edges smooth. Take the stacks apart and discard the tape.

4/To make each cutout in the top back rail, drill a ½"-diameter hole inside the waste. Insert the saber saw blade in the hole and saw out the shape.

4 **Assemble the swing.** Dry assemble the swing to make sure it fits together properly. Then finish sand all the parts. If you plan to paint the glider, apply the first coat *before* the parts are assembled. It will be difficult to get the paint brush into all the nooks and crannies after you put the swing together.

Place the back splats into the grooves in the back rails — do *not* glue them. Let them "float" in the grooves, so they can expand and contract with changes in weather.

Glue the rails into the mortises in the back supports. Since this project will likely be left out in the weather, use waterproof epoxy or resorcinol glue. Reinforce the mortise joints by driving screws through the back supports and into the ends of the rails. Countersink the heads of the screws flush with the surface of the wood.

Assemble the seat rails and seat stiles with glue and screws. Lay the seat slats on the seat frame, spacing them evenly, as shown in the *Side View*. Tack the slats down with finishing nails, but don't drive the nails all the way home until you have all the slats in place. If you need to adjust the positions of the slats to make the spacing more even, you can easily remove the nails. When you're satisfied with the spacing, drive the nails in completely and set the heads.

TRY THIS! Drive each nail at a slight angle and vary the angle forward and back. This will hook the parts together, holding the slats more securely than if you simply drove the nails straight in.

Fasten the back assembly to the seat assembly. Attach the arm supports to the seat, then attach the arms to the arm supports and back. Use both glue and screws to assemble these parts and subassemblies, and countersink the screws.

Finally, attach the braces. Place each brace across the seat rails so the outside edge of the brace is flush with the ends of the rails. Drill ¼"-diameter holes through the braces and rails. Slip a ¼" flat washer over the shank of each eye bolt. Insert the bolt through the hole in the brace and down through the rail. Put another flat washer over the end of the bolt, then secure the bolt with a stop nut. Repeat for all four eye bolts.

5 **Finish the swing.** Round over the edges of the arms, back supports, top back rail, and front seat slat — this will make the swing more comfortable to sit upon. Do any necessary touch-up sanding, then apply paint or another exterior finish to the completed swing.

6 **Hang the swing.** Attach the leaders of the porch swing chains to the eye bolts with S-hooks. Decide where you want to hang the swing — remember, whatever tree or structure you suspend the swing from should be able to support 500–600 pounds. Mount the screw hooks to the underside of a porch rafter, tree limb, or another suitable location. Attach the upper end of the chains to the screw hooks with S-hooks. Adjust the chains so the swing is 16"–17" above the ground or porch floor.

Church Pew

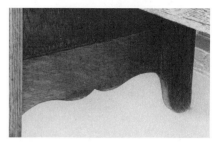

Like deacon's benches, old church pews are sometimes resurrected as outdoor seating. They're often an ideal length, because churches tended to be smaller than they are today and the pews were shorter. They're long enough to comfortably accommodate several people, but they're not so long that they won't fit on a patio or porch.

Often, these pews were handmade by dedicated members of the congregation. The pew shown is one such example — it was apparently built for a church in a midwestern village by a local craftsman. Its unusual joinery tells us that he was more practiced as a carpenter than a furnituremaker.

The marks left by his tools also show that he was accustomed to doing less exacting work. Nonetheless, his commitment made up for his lack of experience. After more than a century, the pew survives.

It also survives because his design is well suited for the out-of-doors — much more so than conventional pew construction. The water runs off the flat seat — there's no curve to hold the water. The arms and the seat frame hold the mortise-and-tenon joinery together, like the keys to a three-dimensional puzzle. This keeps the pew solid, even as the wood expands and contracts with changes in the weather.

Materials List

FINISHED DIMENSIONS

PARTS

A.	Front legs (2)	$1\frac{1}{2}$" x $1\frac{1}{2}$" x 30"
B.	Back legs (2)	$\frac{3}{4}$" x $3\frac{1}{2}$" x $37\frac{1}{2}$"
C.	Arms (2)	$1\frac{1}{2}$" x $1\frac{1}{2}$" x $18\frac{3}{4}$"
D.	Arm gussets (4)	$\frac{3}{4}$" x $1\frac{1}{2}$" x 8"
E.	Top side rails (2)	$\frac{3}{4}$" x 5" x 14"
F.	Bottom side rails (2)	$\frac{3}{4}$" x $3\frac{3}{4}$" x 14"
G.	Side panels (2)	$\frac{1}{4}$" x $7\frac{1}{4}$" x 13"
H.	Front/back apron	$\frac{3}{4}$" x $3\frac{1}{2}$" x $71\frac{1}{4}$"
J.	Seat supports (3)	$1\frac{1}{2}$" x $3\frac{1}{2}$" x $15\frac{3}{4}$"
K.	Seat planks (3)	$\frac{3}{4}$" x $5\frac{13}{16}$" x $70\frac{1}{2}$"
L.	Backrests (2)	$\frac{3}{4}$" x $3\frac{3}{4}$" x $71\frac{1}{4}$"

EXPLODED VIEW

HARDWARE

#10 x 2" Brass flathead wood screws (12)

#10 x $1\frac{1}{4}$" Brass flathead wood screws (18–20)

4d Galvanized finishing nails ($\frac{1}{4}$ lb.)

1

Select the stock and cut the parts to size.

To make this project, you need about 8 board feet of 8/4 (eight-quarters) stock and 26 board feet of 4/4 (four-quarters) stock. You can use almost any cabinet-grade lumber, although church pews were mostly built from oak, chestnut, and walnut. (The pew shown is made from oak.) If you plan to set this pew outside in an unsheltered area, you may want to use an "outdoor" wood such as mahogany, teak, cypress, cedar, or redwood. These have natural oils that make them rot-resistant.

Plane the 8/4 stock to 1½″ thick to make the front legs and arms. Plane 2 board feet of the 4/4 stock to ¼″ thick to make the side panels, and the rest of it to ¾″ thick for the remaining parts. Then cut the parts to the sizes shown in the Materials List.

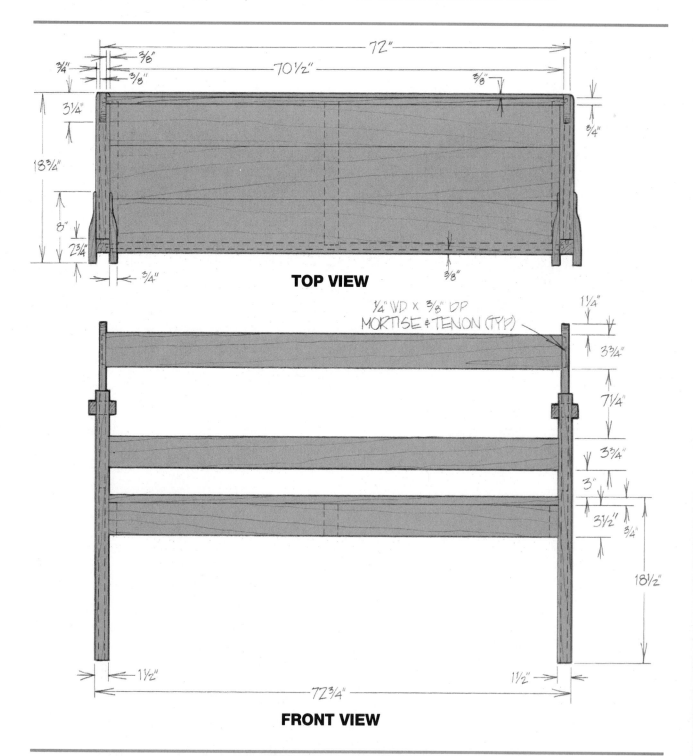

TOP VIEW

FRONT VIEW

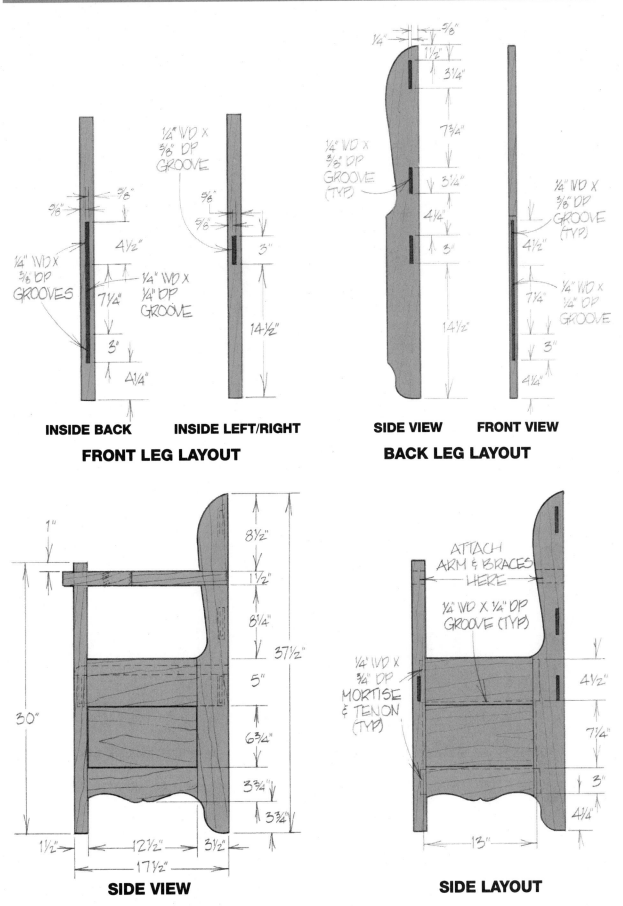

¼" WD X ⅜" DP GROOVE

⅝"

⅝"

4½"

¼" WD X ⅜" DP GROOVES

¼" WD X ¼" DP GROOVE

⅝"

⅝"

3"

7¼"

3"

4¼"

14½"

INSIDE BACK

INSIDE LEFT/RIGHT

FRONT LEG LAYOUT

¼"

⅝"

1½"

3¼"

7¾"

¼" WD X ⅜" DP GROOVE (TYP)

3¼"

4¼"

3"

14½"

¼" WD X ⅜" DP GROOVE (TYP)

4½"

¼" WD X ¼" DP GROOVE

7¼"

3"

4¼"

SIDE VIEW

FRONT VIEW

BACK LEG LAYOUT

1"

8½"

1½"

8¼"

37½"

5"

30"

6¾"

3¾"

3¾"

1½"

12½"

3½"

17½"

SIDE VIEW

ATTACH ARM & BRACES HERE

¼" WD X ¼" DP GROOVE (TYP)

¼" WD X ¾" DP MORTISE & TENON (TYP)

4½"

7¼"

3"

4¼"

13"

SIDE LAYOUT

2 Cut the grooves and mortises in the legs.

The aprons, rails, and backrests all fit into mortises in the legs. The panels rest in grooves in the legs and rails. Lay out the mortises and grooves on the faces and edges of the legs, as shown in the *Front Leg Layout* and *Back Leg Layout*. Cut these grooves and mortises with a hand-held router, then square the blind ends with a chisel. (See Figures 1 through 3.) Also, cut grooves in the bottom edges of the top side rails and the top edges of the bottom side rails. (See Figure 4.)

1/Rout the mortises in the faces of the back legs with a hand-held router and a ¼" straight bit. Stop routing when the bit reaches the marks for the blind ends.

2/To rout the grooves and mortises in the front legs and the edges of the back legs, first clamp scraps of 1½"-thick stock on either side of the boards, as shown. This will provide more support for the router base. Rout the grooves in the legs first, then cut portions of these grooves deeper to make the mortises.

3/After routing all the mortises, square the blind ends with a chisel.

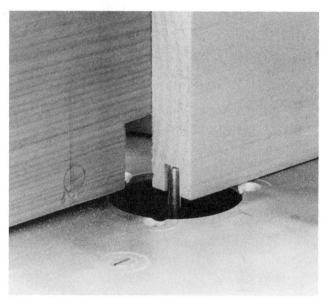

4/Rout the ¼"-wide, ¼"-deep grooves in the edges of the rails. Since these grooves aren't blind, you'll find it easier to cut them with a table-mounted router.

3

Cut the tenons in the aprons, rails, and backrests. Make the tenons to fit the mortises. Using a router and a straight bit, cut ¼″-thick, ¾″- long tenons on the ends of the side rails, and ¼″-thick, ³⁄₈″-long tenons on the ends of the aprons and backrests. (See Figures 5 and 6.)

5/To rout the tenons in the rails, arrange the boards edge to edge. The ends that you wish to cut should be flush with one another. Clamp them to your workbench. Rout a ¼″- deep rabbet in one face of all the rails, turn the boards over, and cut another rabbet. The two rabbets will form a tenon. Use the same method to cut the tenons in the backrests.

6/Cut the shoulders of each tenon with a dovetail saw or coping saw.

4

Cut the dadoes and rabbets in the aprons and seat supports. The seat frame members are joined with dadoes and rabbets. Lay out these joints as shown in the *Seat Frame Layout,* then cut them with a router and straight bit. (See Figure 7.)

7/Rout the dadoes and rabbets using a similar technique to the one you used to make the tenons — clamp the parts edge to edge, then rout them both at the same time.

5

Cut the notches in the arms. The back ends of the arms are notched to fit around the back legs. Lay out these notches as shown in the *Arm Layout,* and cut them with a band saw or saber saw.

TRY THIS! To cut the bottom of each notch, you may find it easier to nibble away the stock, rather than try to turn the blade. Keep the flat of the blade perpendicular to the bottom of the notch and use the teeth like a rasp.

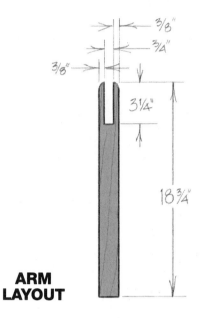

ARM LAYOUT

SEAT FRAME LAYOUT

1½" WD X ¼" DP RABBET (TYP)

1½" WD X ¼" DP DADO

6 Cut the shape of the back legs, bottom side rails, arm gussets, and front seat plank.

Temporarily dry assemble the rails and legs. Enlarge the *Back Leg Pattern* and *Bottom Side Rail Pattern*. Trace these onto the stock, making sure the shapes flow into one another. Also, enlarge the *Arm Gusset Pattern* and trace it onto the stock. Lay out the notches on the front corners of the front seat plank, as shown in the *Front Seat Plank Detail*.

Disassemble the legs and rails. Cut the shapes of the back legs, bottom side rails, arm gussets, and front seat plank with a band saw or saber saw. Sand the sawed edges to remove the saw marks.

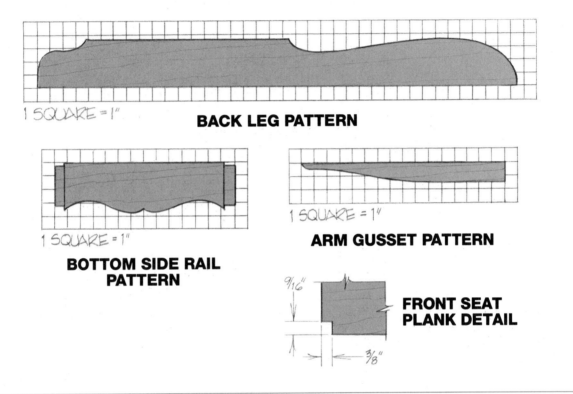

1 SQUARE = 1"

BACK LEG PATTERN

1 SQUARE = 1"

BOTTOM SIDE RAIL PATTERN

1 SQUARE = 1"

ARM GUSSET PATTERN

9/16"   3/8"

FRONT SEAT PLANK DETAIL

7 Assemble the pew.

Finish sand all the parts. Using a waterproof glue such as resorcinol or epoxy, attach the rails to the front legs. Slide the panels in place, then glue the rails to the back legs. Do *not* glue the panels in the grooves; let them float so they can expand and contract.

Glue the notched ends of the arms to the back legs, then glue the arm gussets to the front legs and the front ends of the arm. Reinforce the glue joints with #10 x 1¼" flathead wood screws. Countersink the screws so the heads are flush with the surface of the wood.

Assemble the seat frame with glue and #10 x 2" flathead wood screws. Then assemble the seat frame, side assemblies, and backrests with glue. Reinforce the assembly by attaching the right and left seat supports to the back legs and top side rails with #10 x 2" screws. Again, countersink the heads of all screws.

Attach the seat planks to the seat frame with 4d finishing nails. Drive the nails at a slight angle, and vary the angle left or right with each nail. This will hook the parts together. Set the heads of the nails.

8 Apply a finish to the pew.

Round over the edges of the seat assembly, arms, arm gussets, and backrests. This will make the pew more comfortable to sit upon. Do any necessary touch-up sanding on the pew, then apply an exterior paint or finish. The pew shown is stained and covered with marine spar varnish. Spar varnish provides a clear, durable coat, but it remains elastic so it can expand and contract with the wood.

Deacon's Bench

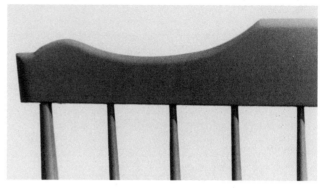

It is unclear how this settee came to be called a "deacon's bench," but the name probably had to do with its use in American churches in the eighteenth and nineteenth centuries. These buildings served many purposes in small rural communities. They weren't just prayer houses. They also doubled as social halls, community centers, and meeting rooms. The furniture in them was mostly seating — various sorts of benches. Unlike modern church pews, these benches weren't fastened down, so they could be rearranged or removed from the churches as needed.

"Windsor" was the most popular clerical furniture style. Windsor benches were light and portable, yet very strong and durable. The congregation sat in long benches, often 12 feet long, or longer, and the clergy rested in shorter ones. Over the years, these shorter pieces became known as deacon's benches.

The bench shown is typical of many built in the early nineteenth century for use in churches and meeting houses. Most of the parts — legs, braces, arm posts, and back spindles — are turned on a lathe. The parts are all mortised and tenoned together. Each of the spindle-turned parts has one or more round tenons which fit into mortise holes.

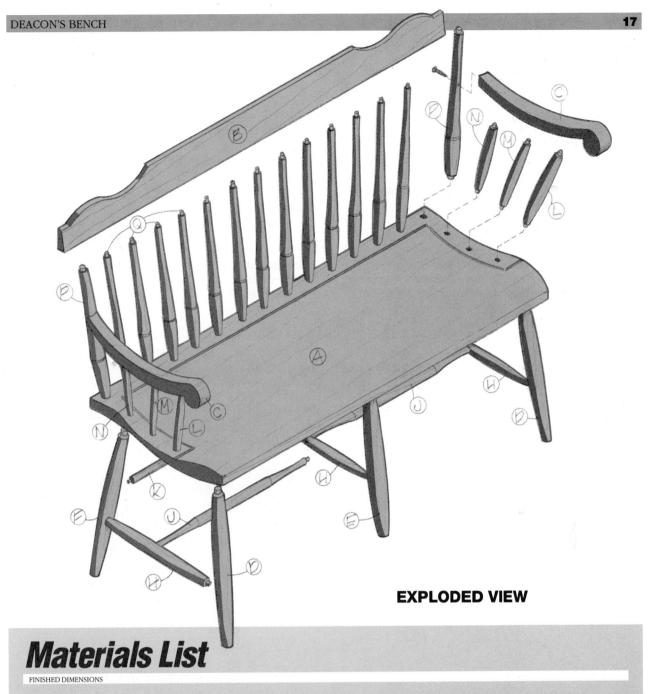

EXPLODED VIEW

Materials List

FINISHED DIMENSIONS

PARTS

A.	Seat	1¼″ x 18⅛″ x 47¾″
B.	Backrest	⅞″ x 4¼″ x 49½″
C.	Arms (2)	1¾″ x 2½″ x 16⅞″
D.	Outside front legs (2)	1¾″ dia. x 16¹⁵/₁₆″
E.	Middle front leg	1¾″ dia. x 16⅞″
F.	Outside back legs (2)	1¾″ dia. x 16¼″
G.	Middle back leg	1¾″ x 16″
H.	Rungs (3)	1⅛″ dia. x 15¹¹/₁₆″
J.	Middle stretchers (2)	1⅛″ dia. x 22⅜″
K.	Back stretchers (2)	⅞″ dia. x 21⅝″
L.	Arm posts (2)	1⅜″ dia. x 11½″
M.	Front arm spindles (2)	1″ dia. x 10⅞″
N.	Back arm spindles (2)	1″ dia. x 10⅜″
P.	Back posts (2)	1¼″ dia. x 16⅝″
Q.	Back spindles (13)	1″ dia. x 16½″

HARDWARE

#10 x 1¾″ Flathead wood screws (2)

1

Select the stock and cut the parts to size. To make this project, you need about 20 board feet of 6/4 (six-quarters) stock, and about 5 board feet of 8/4 (eight-quarters) stock. A piece of Windsor furniture was typically made from several different types of wood. Eighteenth- and nineteenth-century American craftsmen made the seat from pine or poplar, the backrest and arms from hickory, chestnut, oak, or ash, and the legs, rungs, back spindles, and other turned parts from maple or birch. (The completed piece was usually painted to disguise the mismatched wood grains.) On the bench shown, the seat is made of pine and all the other parts are maple.

Select the seat lumber from the 6/4 stock, and plane it to $1\frac{1}{4}''$ thick. If necessary, plane narrow boards and glue them together to make a single board at least $18\frac{1}{8}''$ wide. From the same stock, select the backrest and plane it to $\frac{7}{8}''$ thick. From the 8/4 stock, select the wood for the arms, then plane it to $1\frac{3}{4}''$ thick. Cut the seat, backrest, and arms to the sizes given in the Materials List.

Cut the remainder of the stock into turning blocks to make the legs, rungs, stretchers, posts, and spindles. Each block should be about $\frac{1}{4}''$ wider and thicker and $1''$ longer than the finished dimensions of the turning. This will give you a little extra stock with which to mount the wood on the lathe and turn it to the proper diameter.

2

Drill the round mortises in the seat, backrest, and arms. All the spindles, posts, and legs are mounted in round mortises in the seat, backrest, or arms. Most of these mortises are drilled at angles, many of them at *compound* angles. Carefully check the angles on the drawings before you drill each mortise hole. Where possible, draw a guideline when you mark the location of a mortise to show how to angle it. (See Figure 1.) When you drill the mortise, use a hand-held power drill and line up the bit with the guidelines. (See Figure 2.) To gauge the depth of each hole, use stop collars if you have them. If not, simply wrap masking tape around the bit to indicate when to stop drilling. (See Figure 3.)

1/Many of the round mortises in this project are drilled at different angles. To avoid confusion, mark the angle when you mark the location of the hole. If possible, draw a guideline to show which direction to angle the hole.

2/When you drill a mortise, align the bit with the guideline. Don't worry if the alignment isn't precise — the angles aren't critical.

3/Use stop collars to automatically stop the drill at the proper depth. If you don't have stop collars, wrap masking tape around the bit and stop drilling when the leading edge of the tape reaches the surface of the wood.

Note: While the round mortises are drilled at many different angles in this project, none of the angles is critical. You can be several degrees off, and the parts will still fit reasonably well. (In fact, the construction may actually be tighter if all the angles aren't precise.) Old-time Windsor chairmakers simply eyeballed the angles of their mortises.

Begin with the backrest — it's the simplest. Mark the locations and angles for fifteen mortise holes along the bottom edge, as shown in the *Backrest Layout*. Thirteen are ¼″ diameter and ½″ deep; the outer two are ⅝″ diameter and ½″ deep. Note that the center hole in the

backrest is square to the edge, while all the others are angled either left or right. Finally, drill the holes.

Enlarge the *Arm Layout and Pattern/Side View*. Trace the pattern and the profile of the ¾″-diameter mortises onto one face of the arm stock. Mark the positions of the mortises on the bottom edge, as shown in the *Arm Layout and Pattern/Bottom View*. Drill each mortise at the angle shown and set the stop collar so the drill will cut through the waste and into the arm. Later, when you saw out the shapes of the arms, the mortises will be at the proper depths and angles.

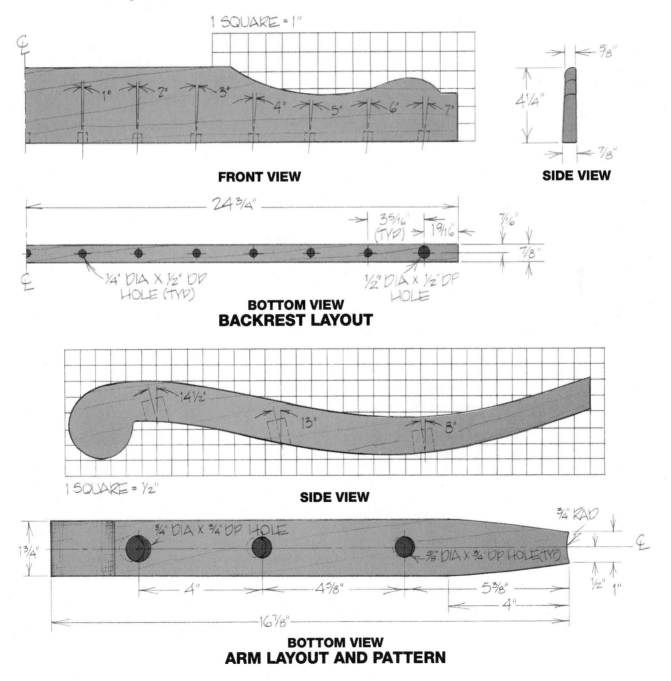

FRONT VIEW

SIDE VIEW

BOTTOM VIEW
BACKREST LAYOUT

SIDE VIEW

BOTTOM VIEW
ARM LAYOUT AND PATTERN

Enlarge the *Seat Pattern* and trace it onto the seat stock. (Save the pattern. You'll need it again later.) Mark the locations of the ½"-diameter, ⅝"-diameter, and ¾"-diameter mortises on the top surface, as shown on the *Seat Layout/Top View,* then turn the seat over and mark the locations of the ⅞"-diameter mortises, as shown on the *Seat Layout/Bottom View.* When making these mortises, remember that most of them must be drilled at *compound* angles — not only do you have to angle the drill bit side-to-side, but also back-to-front. Consult the *Seat Layout/Back View* for the side to side angles, and the *Seat Layout/Side View* for the back to front angles.

TRY THIS! Although you can mark guidelines on the edge of the seat to aid in drilling the mortises, they will be difficult to see. To help eyeball the angles — especially the compound angles — mount a 4"-long piece of coat-hanger wire in a small piece of scrap wood. With the aid of a protractor, bend the wire to the proper angle. Before drilling each mortise, place the wire a few inches away. Align the bit as closely as possible with the wire as you drill.

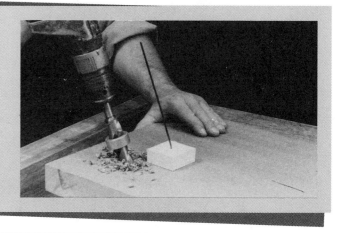

3 **Scoop the seat.** Scooping the seat involves extensive handwork, but portions can be done with power tools. Enlarge the *Seat Profile* and trace it onto *both* ends of the stock — this will give you a reference as you work. Using a table saw, make a series of overlapping cove cuts to remove as much of the waste as possible. (See Figure 4.) Plane, scrape, and sand the stock until the seat reaches the desired contour. As you work, clamp a long, straight board to the seat to preserve a straight, distinct line between the flat area and the scooped area. (See Figure 5.) Without the board, you might round over portions of the flat area while scraping and sanding, making the scoop look sloppy.

4/Rough out the scooped seat by making overlapping cove cuts with a table saw. Clamp a straightedge to the worktable to guide the work, then feed the seat across the blade at a 45° angle. Take small bites, cutting just ¹⁄₁₆"–⅛" deeper with each pass until the cove reaches the required depth.

5/While you're shaping and smoothing the scooped portion of the seat, preserve the hard line between the flat and curved areas by clamping a board to the stock.

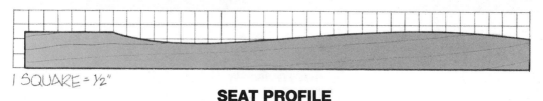

I SQUARE = ½"

SEAT PROFILE

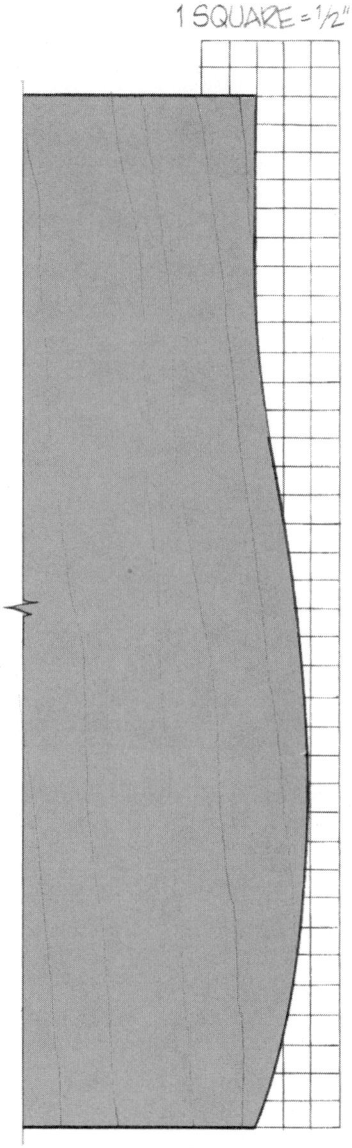
1 SQUARE = 1/2"

SEAT PATTERN

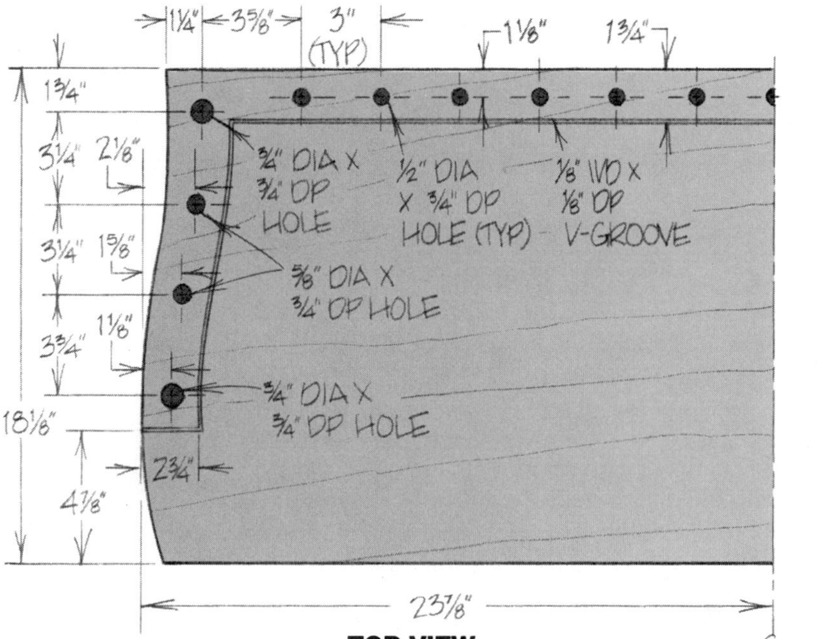
1 1/4"
3 5/8"
3" (TYP)
1 1/8"
1 3/4"
1 3/4"
3 1/4"
2 1/8"
3 1/4"
1 5/8"
3 3/4"
1 1/8"
18 1/8"
4 1/8"
2 3/4"
3/4" DIA X 3/4" DP HOLE
1/2" DIA X 3/4" DP HOLE (TYP)
1/8" WD X 1/8" DP V-GROOVE
5/8" DIA X 3/4" DP HOLE
3/4" DIA X 3/4" DP HOLE
23 7/8"

TOP VIEW

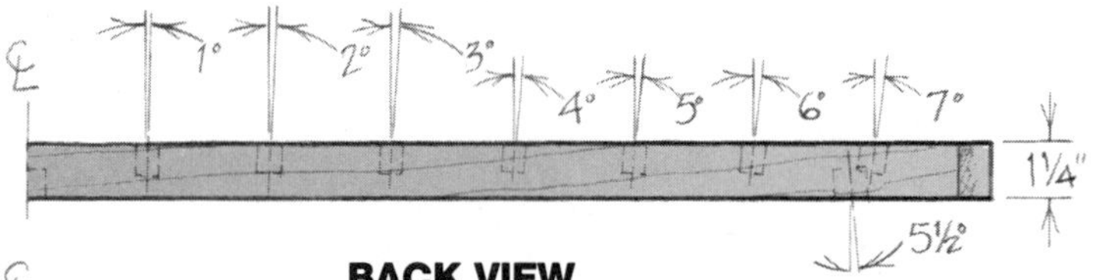
1°
2°
3°
4°
5°
6°
7°
1 1/4"
5 1/2°

BACK VIEW

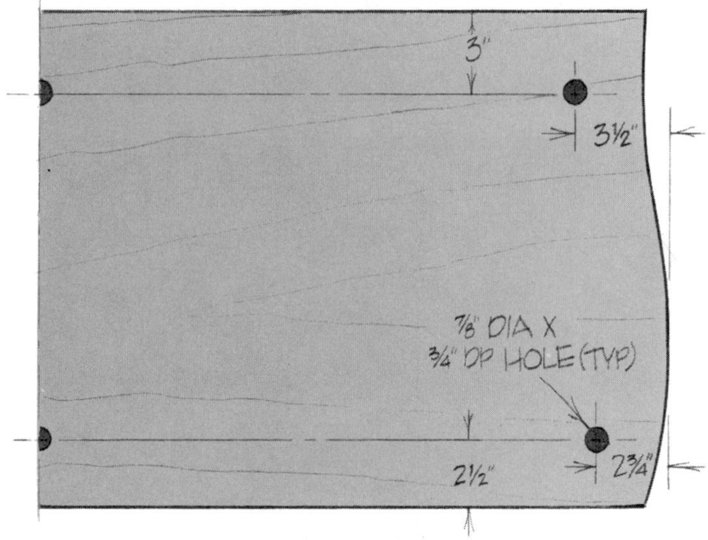
3"
3 1/2"
7/8" DIA X 3/4" DP HOLE (TYP)
2 1/2"
2 3/4"

BOTTOM VIEW

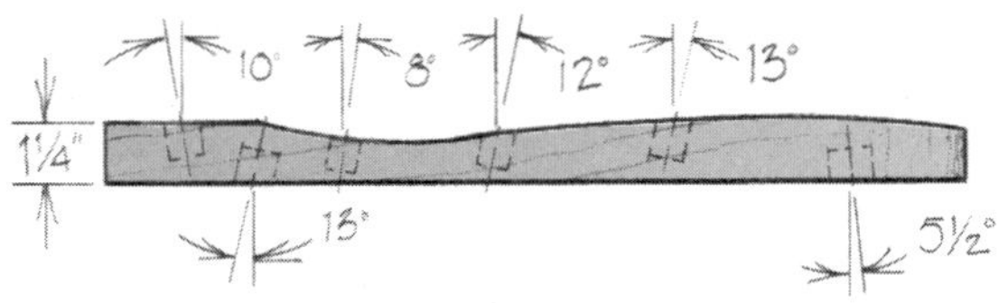
10°
8°
12°
13°
1 1/4"
13°
5 1/2°

SIDE VIEW

SEAT LAYOUT

4

Taper the backrest. As shown in the *Side View*, the backrest tapers from $^7/_8''$ at the bottom edge to $^5/_8''$ at the top. To make this taper, cut a $^1/_4''$ spacer, $^3/_4''$ wide and as long as the backrest. Temporarily stick this spacer to one face of the backrest with double-faced carpet tape, flush with the top edge. Run the backrest through a planer with the spacer down. Make several passes, removing about $^1/_{16}''$ of stock with each pass until you cut the taper completely. (See Figure 6.) Remove and discard the spacer and tape.

6/Cut the taper in the backrest on a planer. Tape a spacer to the back side of the wood to hold the other side at an angle to the planer knives. Then run the backrest through the planer.

5

Cut the shape of the seat, backrest, and the arms. Since most of the seat pattern was removed when you scooped the seat, trace it on the stock again. Also, enlarge the backrest pattern, as shown in the *Backrest Layout/Front View*. Trace the pattern onto the backrest stock.

Cut the shapes of the seat, backrest, and arms with a saber saw, band saw, or fretsaw. Also round over the top of the backrest, using a spokeshave and chisels. (Note that only the front top edge is rounded.) Sand the sawed and rounded areas smooth.

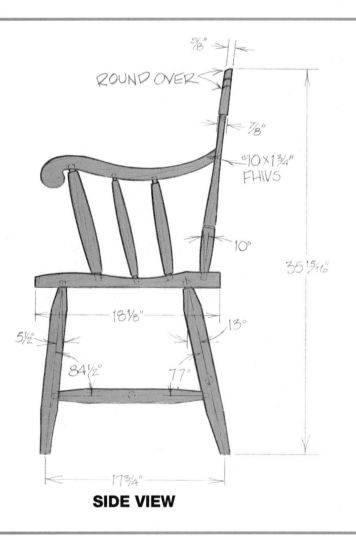

SIDE VIEW

6

Turn the legs, stretchers, rungs, posts, and spindles. Turn all the round parts — legs, stretchers, rungs, posts, and spindles — on a lathe. As precisely as possible, follow the contours shown in the *Outside Front Leg Layout, Outside Back Leg Layout, Middle Front Leg Layout, Middle Back Leg Layout, Middle Stretcher Layout, Back Stretcher Layout, Rung Layout, Arm Post Layout, Front Arm Spindle Layout, Back Arm Spindle Layout, Back Post Layout,* and *Back Spindle Layout.* Use a steadyrest to keep the long, slender parts such as the back spindles from whipping as you turn them. (See Figure 7.)

Be especially careful when making the tenons on these parts — they must fit the round mortises precisely. A loose joint will be weak and it will grow weaker each time you sit on the bench.

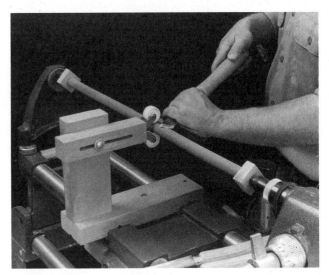

7/Long, slender turnings may whip or bow as you work them. To prevent this, don't put too much pressure between the drive center and the tailstock. Also, use a steadyrest to support the spindle between the centers.

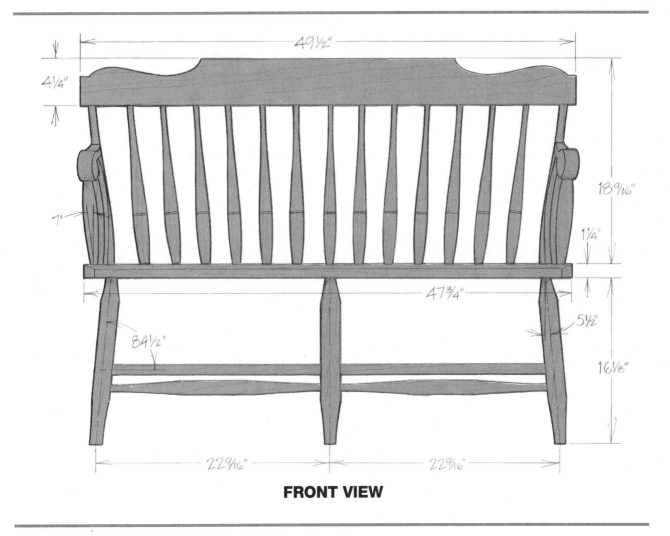

FRONT VIEW

To cut the tenons to the proper diameters, make several gauges, one for each size of tenon. To make a gauge, drill a hole in a piece of scrap wood using the same bit you used to bore the mortise. Cut a slot from the outside edge of the scrap into the hole. Carefully rasp away the edges of the slot until it's *precisely* as wide as the tenon you want to make. Turn each tenon until it's *slightly* larger than needed. Hold the tenon gauge against the tenon from one side while you sand the tenon from the other. (See Figure 8.) When the gauge slips over the tenon, stop sanding *immediately* — the tenon diameter is correct.

When you finish turning each part, finish sand it on the lathe. Mark the position of any mortise holes on the turnings.

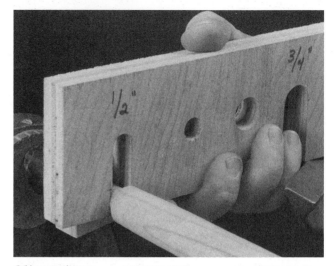

8/Use sandpaper to remove the last little bit of stock from the diameter of each tenon. Sandpaper removes stock more slowly than a chisel and there's less chance you'll cut the tenon too small. As you work, use a homemade tenon gauge to measure the precise diameter of the tenon.

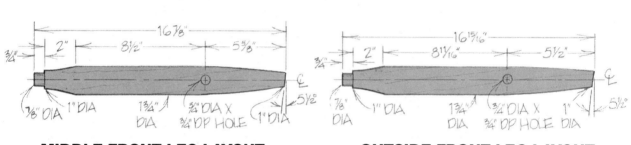

MIDDLE FRONT LEG LAYOUT

OUTSIDE FRONT LEG LAYOUT

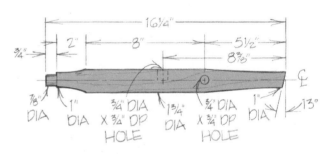

MIDDLE BACK LEG LAYOUT

OUTSIDE BACK LEG LAYOUT

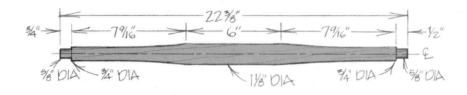

MIDDLE STRETCHER LAYOUT

7 Drill mortises for rungs and stretchers.

Drill round mortises in the legs for the rungs and back stretchers. Drill mortises in the rungs for the middle stretchers. Note that some of these holes must be angled. Consult the *Front View* and *Side View* to find the angles. To hold these round parts while you drill them, place them in a V-jig.

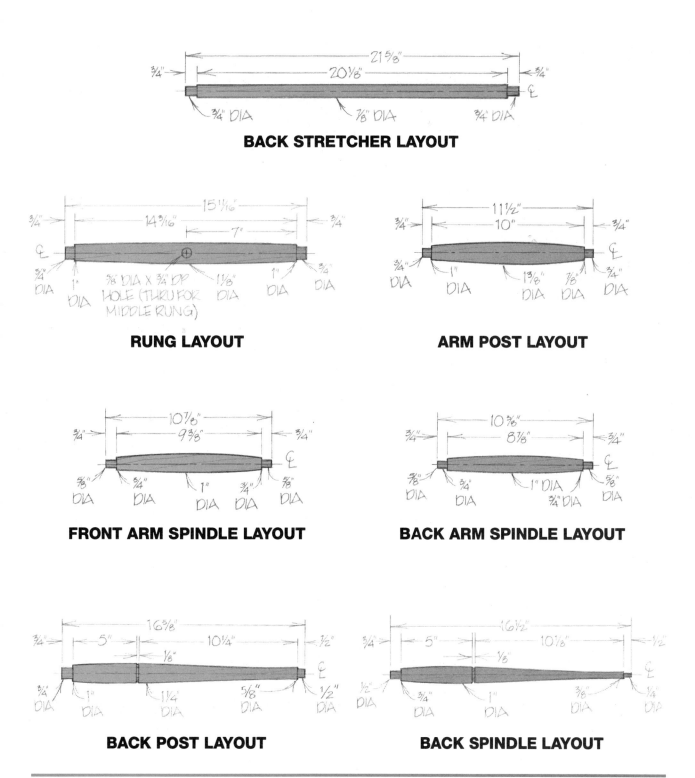

BACK STRETCHER LAYOUT

RUNG LAYOUT

ARM POST LAYOUT

FRONT ARM SPINDLE LAYOUT

BACK ARM SPINDLE LAYOUT

BACK POST LAYOUT

BACK SPINDLE LAYOUT

8 **Cut the groove in the seat.** As mentioned previously, Windsor furniture was often painted to hide the mismatched wood. However, some makers left the seat partially unpainted. Since the paint would eventually wear off, they finished the seat with oil or clear varnish — something that wouldn't show the wear so plainly. To separate the painted areas from the un-painted, they sometimes cut a decorative groove in the top surface of the seat.

Lay out the 1/8"-wide, 1/8"-deep V-groove in the seat, as shown in the *Seat Layout/Top View.* Cut this groove with a router and a V-groove bit, or carve it with a V-shaped chisel (sometimes called a *veiner*).

TRY THIS! To carve the groove with a veiner, you may have to regrind your chisel. Typically, veiner chisels are ground at the factory so the "nose" or bottom part of the V leads the sides slightly. This profile works well for many woodworking operations, but not for carving. You'll find the chisel will cut with the grain easily enough, but not cross-grain. To get a veiner to cut with the grain *and* cross-grain with equal ease, regrind the profile so the slides lead the nose.

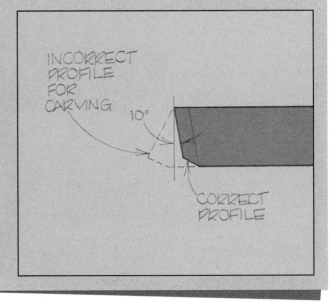

9 **Assemble the bench.** Dry assemble all the parts to be sure that they fit together correctly. You may have to trim them to length, enlarge mortises, or shim tenons to get all the parts to fit snugly. When you're satisfied with the fit, disassemble the bench and finish sand any parts that may still need it — seat, back-rest, and arms.

Glue the legs and the rungs together so you have three leg/rung assemblies. Glue the stretchers to the legs and rungs, joining the assemblies. Then glue the legs into the seat — back legs first, then front legs.

Note: You must assemble all these parts before the glue dries, while the joints are still flexible. It's much harder to assemble the bench after the joints become rigid.

Turn the seat right side up, resting it on its legs. If necessary, trim the bottom of the legs so the bench sits solidly on the floor. Glue the back posts and back spindles in the seat, then glue them in the backrest. Glue the arm posts and arm spindles in the arms, then glue the arm assemblies in the seat. Attach the arms to the back post with flathead wood screws, driving the screws through the posts and into the ends of the arms. Countersink the heads of the screws.

10 **Finish the bench.** Do any necessary touch-up sanding. Finish the top surface of the seat (inside and in front of the groove) with stain and varnish. Let the varnish dry, then mask off the finished side of the groove.

Paint the rest of the bench. Traditionally, these benches were painted green or red, but you can use any color that suits your fancy. You may also want to stencil or paint a design on the backrest.

Let the paint dry, then paint the groove black. (Some makers gilded the grooves on their benches.) This will help delineate the separation between the painted area of the seat from the finished area.

Hobby Horse Glider

Here's a ride on the wild side for kids — a hobby horse glider. Hang the glider from a tree, porch roof, gym set, or any sturdy structure. To set it in motion, the child presses forward and then pulls back on the handhold. As the glider begins to move, the head will tilt back and forth while the seat remains level.

This ingenious plaything also has a built-in safety feature. You can limit the travel of the glider simply by shortening or lengthening the ropes. The shorter the ropes, the less the glider will travel forward and back — and the closer it will remain to the ground. For a young child, hang the glider from a low structure using ropes that are only 3' or 4' long. As the child grows, attach it to higher frames using longer ropes.

Note: This project is *not* recommended for children who are younger than five years old or physically handicapped.

Materials List

FINISHED DIMENSIONS

PARTS

A. Vertical support   1³/₄″ x 4″ x 24″
B. Horizontal
support   1³/₄″ x 1³/₄″ x 25¹/₂″
C. Seat   ³/₄″ x 7″ x 7″
D. Handhold/
footrest (2)   1″ dia. x 18″
E. Pivot   1″ dia. x 4″

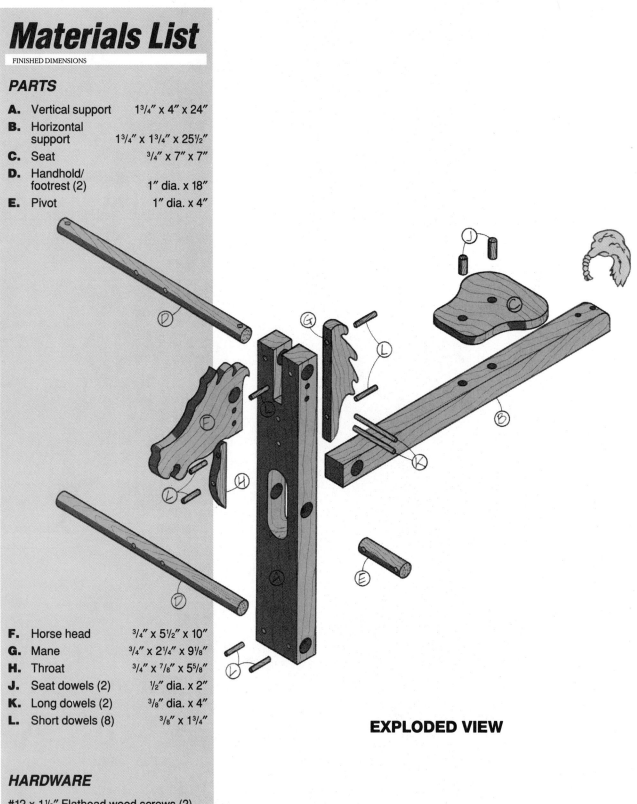

F. Horse head   ³/₄″ x 5¹/₂″ x 10″
G. Mane   ³/₄″ x 2¹/₄″ x 9¹/₈″
H. Throat   ³/₄″ x ⁷/₈″ x 5⁵/₈″
J. Seat dowels (2)   ¹/₂″ dia. x 2″
K. Long dowels (2)   ³/₈″ dia. x 4″
L. Short dowels (8)   ³/₈″ x 1³/₄″

EXPLODED VIEW

HARDWARE

#12 x 1¹/₂″ Flathead wood screws (2)
³/₈″ Manila rope (20′–30′)
1″ Manila rope (12″)

1

Select the stock and cut the parts to size. To make this project, you need about 3 board feet of 8/4 (eight-quarters) stock, 2 board feet of 4/4 (four-quarters) stock, 4 feet of 1"-diameter dowel rod, and 2 feet of ³/₈" dowel rod. Since this project will likely see heavy use (and abuse), choose an extremely hard wood, such as oak, maple, birch, or hickory. You can also use teak — it weathers well. The glider shown is made of oak.

Plane the 8/4 stock to 1³/₄" thick, and the 4/4 stock to ³/₄" thick. Cut the vertical and horizontal supports, pivot, handhold, and footrest to size. Cut the dowels ¹/₁₆"–¹/₈" longer than specified. Don't cut the shaped parts (seat, head, mane, and throat) until later.

2

Cut the joinery. The glider requires only two joints other than butt joints: The horse head is mounted in a slot; and the horizontal and vertical supports are joined by a pivot housed in a through mortise. Both of these joints are cut in the vertical support.

Lay out the slot and the mortise as shown in the *Vertical Support Layout*. Cut the slot with a band saw or saber saw. You may have to nibble away the waste at the bottom of the slot if you don't have room to make the turn. (See Figure 1.)

To make the mortise, bore two 2"-diameter holes, 3¹/₂" apart, with a hole saw. Using a saber saw or a coping saw, cut away the waste between the holes. (See Figure 2.) Clean up the edges of the mortise with a file.

1/When cutting long, narrow, slots, you don't always have room to turn the blade and cut the bottom. If this is the case, use the blade like a rasp. With the teeth, nibble away the waste at the bottom of the slot.

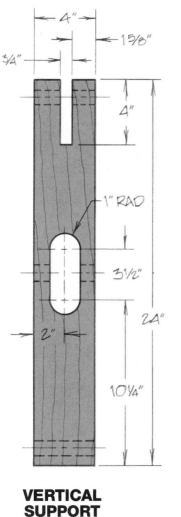

4"
1⅝"
¾"
4"
1" RAD
3½"
2"
24"
10¼"

**VERTICAL
SUPPORT
LAYOUT**

2/To make the mortise that houses the pivot, first drill two large holes. Then cut away the waste between the holes.

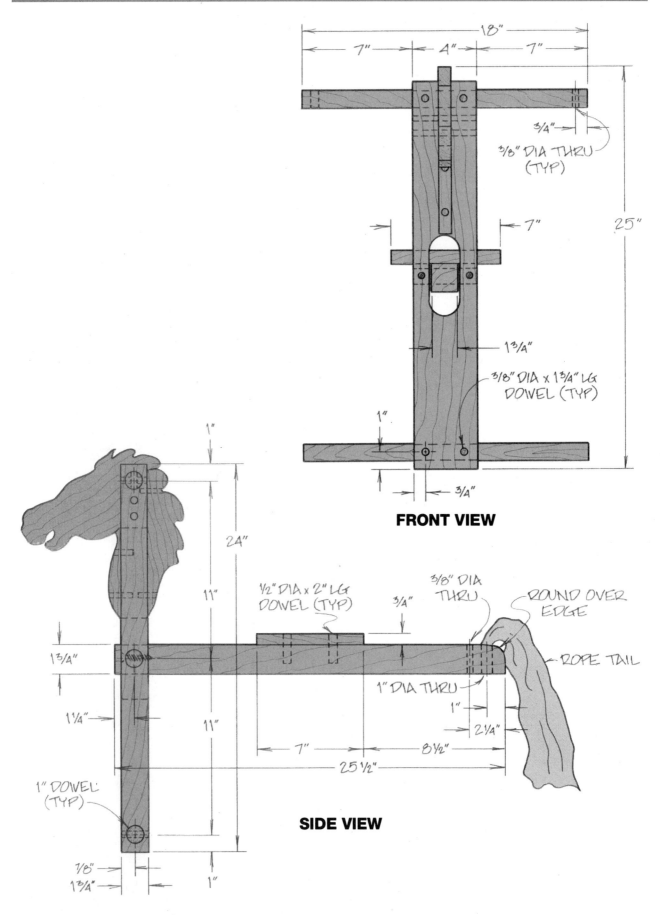

FRONT VIEW

SIDE VIEW

3 Cut the shapes of the horse and seat.

Enlarge the *Horse Pattern* and *Seat Pattern,* and trace the shapes onto the ³/₄″-thick stock. Pay careful attention to the grain direction shown on the patterns. Cut the head, mane, throat, and seat shapes with a band saw or saber saw, then sand the sawed edges.

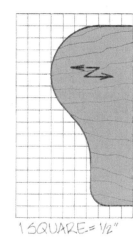

SEAT PATTERN

1 SQUARE = ½″

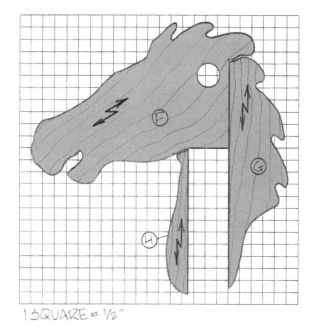

1 SQUARE = ½″

HORSE PATTERN

4 Drill the holes.

Drill 1″-diameter holes in the edges of the vertical and horizontal supports, as shown in the *Side View,* for the handhold, footrest, and pivot. Position the head in the slot. Using the handhold hole as a guide, drill a 1″-diameter hole through the head. Also, drill a 1″-diameter hole through the face of the horizontal support, near the back end, to mount the rope tail.

Remove the 1″ bit from the drill and replace it with a ³/₈″ bit. Temporarily put the handhold in place to hold the head in the slot. Drill two ³/₈″-diameter holes through the edge of the vertical support and head for the long dowels.

Clamp the vertical support to the workbench with the head hanging over the edge, nose down. Hold the mane in place and drill two ³/₈″-diameter, 1³/₄″-deep holes through the mane and into the support. (See Figure 3.) Turn the head over and do the same for the throat.

Drill ³/₈″-diameter holes for the ropes near each end of the handhold and the back end of the horizontal support. (Secure the handhold in a V-jig to keep it from turning as you drill it.) Remove the head, mane, and throat from the vertical support. Slide the handhold and footrest into place. Make sure the rope holes in the handhold are *parallel* to the long dimension of the sup-

port. Drill two ³/₈″-diameter dowel holes through the support and the handhold, as shown in the *Front View.* Do the same for the footrest.

Change to a ¹/₂″ drill bit. Place the seat on the top face of the horizontal support. Drill two ¹/₂″-diameter, 2″-deep dowel holes through the seat and into the support. If needed, use double-faced carpet tape to keep the parts from shifting while you drill.

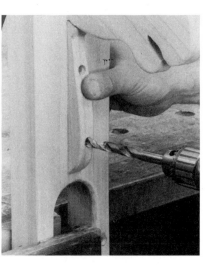

3/Drill dowel holes through the mane and throat and into the vertical support. If necessary, use double-faced carpet tape to keep the parts from shifting while you drill them.

5 Assemble the glider. Finish sand all the parts. Assemble the vertical support, handhold, footrest, head, mane, and throat with dowels and glue. Also, assemble the horizontal support and seat. Since this project will likely be left out in the weather, use a waterproof glue such as resorcinol or epoxy. Let the glue dry, then sand or file the ends of the dowels flush with the surface of the wood.

Slide the front end of the horizontal support into the mortise in the vertical support. Insert the pivot through the supports. Drive wood screws through the vertical support and into the pivot, on either side of the mortise. Countersink the screws so the heads are flush with the wood surface.

Note: Leave the heads of the screws accessible so you can easily replace the pivot if it becomes worn.

6 Paint the glider. Remove the screws, slide the pivot out of its holes, and take the horizontal and vertical supports apart. Do any necessary touch-up sanding, then paint or finish the glider. Do *not* paint or finish the pivot or the insides of the pivot holes. When the paint or finish dries, reassemble the glider.

7 Install the rope tail. Cut a 12"-long piece of 1" Manila rope. Apply waterproof glue to one end and insert it down through the 1"-diameter hole in the horizontal support. Let $1/8$"–$1/4$" protrude from the bottom of the hole — most of the rope must stick out of the top. The fit should be snug enough that the rope will stay in place without the glue. If the fit is too loose, shim the rope with wooden wedges.

Let the glue dry, then cut the rope flush with the bottom face of the support. Unravel the portion of the rope that protrudes from the top. (See Figure 4.)

Note: Most hardware stores do not carry 1" Manila rope; you may have to purchase it from a marine supply store or another industrial supplier. You can also use several 12" lengths of $1/2$" or $3/8$" rope, bound together.

4/To make the rope tail look like a tail, you must unravel the rope. Untwist the strands, then separate each strand into the individual Manila fibers.

8 Hang the glider. Insert $3/8$" Manila rope down through the $3/8$"-diameter rope holes in the handhold and horizontal support. Tie overhand knots in the ends of the ropes to prevent them from slipping out of the holes, then apply a little glue to the knots to keep them from coming undone.

Install three eye screws in a tree limb, gym set frame, porch roof, or another structure to support the glider. These screws should be spaced *approximately* the same as the rope holes. However, it won't matter if the spacing is off several inches.

Insert the ropes through the eye screws. Adjust the lengths so the footrest is 4"–6" off the ground and the horizontal support is level. Tie off the ropes and apply a little glue to the knots.

TRY THIS! For very young children, you may want to space the eye screws for the support ropes much further apart than the rope holes — perhaps as much as several *feet* further apart. This will limit the travel of the glider and make it more stable.

Making Long-Lasting Pivot Joints

Swings, gliders, and other outdoor furniture often incorporate pivot joints. In this book, both the Lawn Glider and the Hobby Horse Glider have parts that pivot as the gliders swing back and forth. The Folding Bench collapses on itself, then opens out again. These moving joints see a lot of use, much more so than other parts of the project — and they tend to wear out much faster.

There are several important things you can do to prolong the life of pivot joints:

■ *Eliminate as much friction as possible.* Rough, dry wood wears very fast because it generates friction as the parts rub together. To prevent this, make the parts of the joints as smooth as possible. Finish sand the surfaces *inside* the joints just as you do the surfaces on the outside of the project. Apply a thick coat of paste wax or paraffin wax to lubricate these surfaces before you assemble the parts.

■ *Use hard materials, if possible.* Pivots made of oak, maple, birch, and other hard, dense woods wear much longer than pivots of softer woods. Unfortunately, most weather-resistant woods are not hard. Cypress, redwood, cedar, and pressure-treated pine are all very soft. Mahogany, even though it's a hardwood, is softer than most. Only teak is as hard as maple or oak.

■ *Don't use bolts or rods with threads* inside *pivots.* If you use a bolt as a pivot, choose one with a smooth shank that's only threaded on the end. The portion of the bolt inside the joint must not be rough. Threaded bolts and rods will eat away the wood surrounding a pivot like saw teeth.

■ *Keep the wooden parts from rubbing.* Whenever you can, prevent the wooden parts from touching one another. Keep them apart with flat washers or fender washers so the faces don't rub. You can also keep them from rubbing on the pivot by making a metal *bushing*.

For instance, if you wish to use a ¼″-diameter carriage bolt for a pivot, find a *roll pin* or *pipe nipple* with an inside diameter that's slightly larger than ¼″. (See Figure A.) It won't matter if there's a little slop. Drill the pivot hole in the wood to fit the outside diameter of the pin or pipe.

Cut the roll pin or pipe nipple to the same length as the pivot hole. Press the metal part into the wood so the ends are flush with the outside surfaces. (See Figure B.) Then insert the carriage bolt through it. The roll pin or pipe nipple will form a metal sleeve or bushing. (See Figure C.) When the pivot is in motion, the carriage bolt will rub on this sleeve — not on the wood.

B/Cut the roll pin or pipe nipple to length with a hacksaw, then drive it into the pivot hole. The fit should be snug, but not too tight. If it's too loose, secure it with epoxy glue.

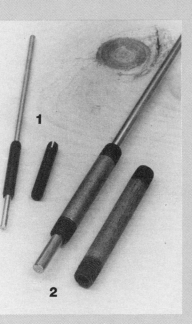

A/You can make your own metal bushing from an inexpensive roll pin (1) or pipe nipple (2). Choose hardware that fits over the pivot bolt without binding.

C/To be properly installed, the pin or pipe must line the hole completely. The ends of the metal part should be flush with the surfaces of the board.

Slab-End Bench

S lab-end benches and stools first appeared in the fifteenth century. Each piece consisted of a sawn plank or "slab" top supported by two vertical slabs. The supporting slabs were braced by rails or stretchers. A few, like the bench shown, incor- porated both rails and stretchers. It's a simple construction method by our standards, but it was elegant in its time. Saw- mills had only just been invented (the first was built in 1320), and furni- ture made of flat boards was still a luxury.

Early slab-end benches were inspired by the Gothic architecture of medieval times, and they could be very ornate. But as the design became popular (and sawed boards became less expensive), common folks simplified it to suit their skills and tastes. The slab-end bench even- tually became a country piece, and the slabs were left plain or cut with folk motifs. The country-style bench shown was designed and built by Gary Simon of West Milton, Ohio.

Materials List

FINISHED DIMENSIONS

PARTS

A. Seat   3/4" x 11 1/4" x 72"
B. Legs (2)   3/4" x 9 3/4" x 16 1/4"
C. Rails (2)   3/4" x 2 1/2" x 72"
D. Stretcher   3/4" x 7 1/4" x 62 1/2"

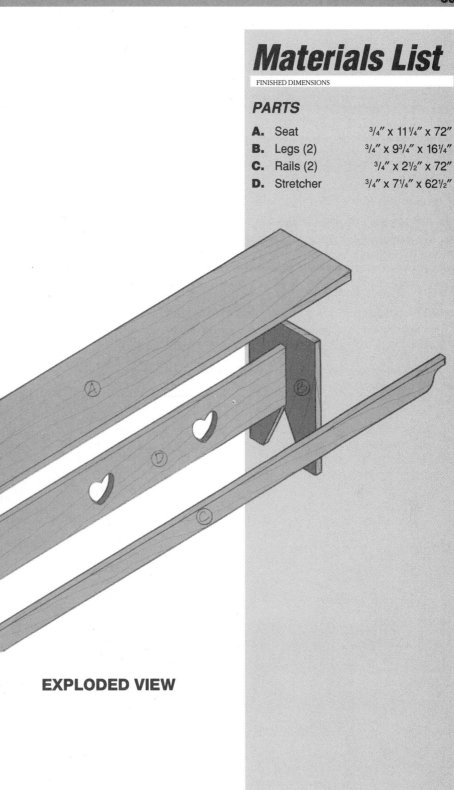

EXPLODED VIEW

HARDWARE

8d Galvanized spiral decking nails
  (1/4 lb.)

1

Select the stock and cut the parts to size. To make this project, you need about 18 board feet of 4/4 (four-quarters) stock. You can use almost any cabinet-grade wood. Early slab-end benches were made of oak; later, they were built mostly of maple, poplar, and pine. You can also use construction-grade 1 x 12 lumber, if you select boards with solid knots and no splits. The bench shown is made from #2 common pine shelving stock.

Plane the stock to ¾″ thick, if necessary. Then cut the parts to the sizes shown in the Materials List.

2

Cut the shapes of the legs and rails. Arrange the boards in two stacks, one for the rails and the other for the legs. Tape the stacks together with all ends and edges flush. Enlarge the *Rail Pattern* and trace it onto the top board in the rail stack. Also, lay out the shape of the legs, as shown in the *End View,* on the top board in the leg stack.

Cut the shapes with a band saw or saber saw, and sand the sawed edges. Take the stacks apart and discard the tape.

3

Make the cutouts in the stretcher. Enlarge the *Heart Pattern* and trace it onto the stretcher, as shown in the *Front View.* Drill a hole through the waste of each cutout. Insert the blade of a saber saw or coping saw into the hole, cut to the pattern line, then cut away the waste. Sand the sawed edges inside the cutout. (See Figure 1.)

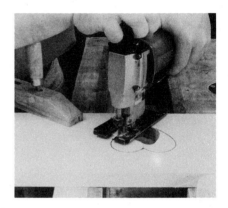

1/To make a cutout, first drill a hole through the waste. Insert the blade of a saber saw or coping saw through this hole, and saw the shape of the cutout.

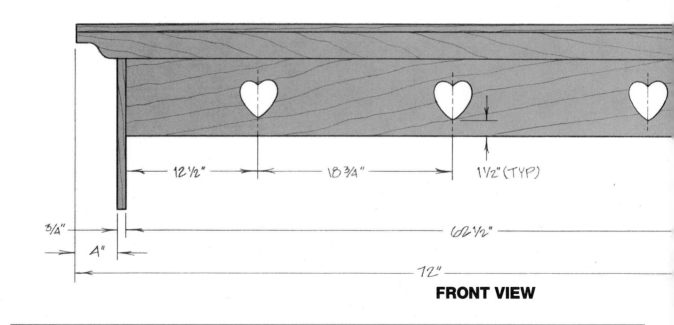

FRONT VIEW

4 **Assemble the bench.** Finish sand all the parts. Fasten the stretcher to the legs, using spiral nails. Then add the rails and seat. Drill pilot holes for the nails before you drive them; this will keep them from splitting the wood. Don't drive the nails all the way home until you've assembled all the parts, so you can remove the nails if necessary.

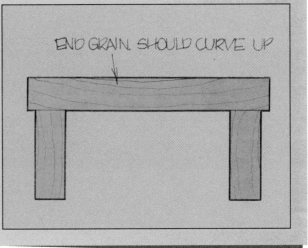

TRY THIS!   When you attach the seat, turn it so the annual rings on the ends of the board curve *up*. Wood tends to cup in the direction opposite the annual rings' curve. If the seat should cup, the water will run off the bench.

5 **Finish the bench.** Do any necessary touch-up sanding on the bench, then apply an exterior paint or finish. Traditionally, these benches were finished with milk paint. You can duplicate the look of milk paint by applying a flat latex paint, letting it dry, then covering the latex with a coat of boiled linseed oil.

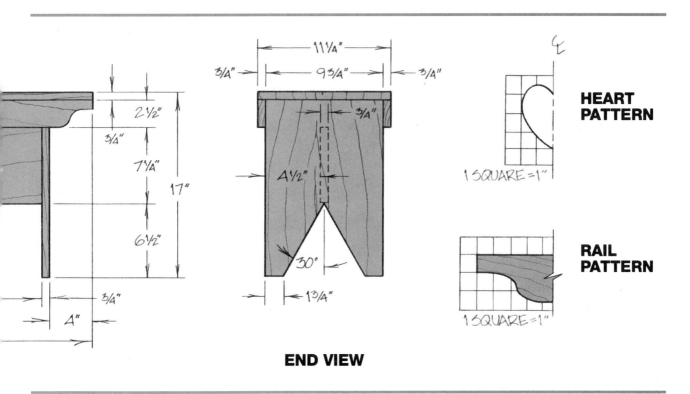

HEART PATTERN

1 SQUARE = 1"

RAIL PATTERN

1 SQUARE = 1"

END VIEW

Folding Bench

Collapsible furniture
dates back to the time of
the Romans, when
magistrates and ministers
traveled from province to
province, holding court.
They carried their court
seating with them —
X-shaped folding benches
and chairs called
"curules." This collapsible
outdoor bench is reminis-
cent of those ancient
Roman designs. The

X-shaped legs fold up in
a similar way. You simply
pull up on the seat, and
the legs collapse like
scissors.

The bench also offers
many of the same advan-

tages as the old-time
curules. It's comfortable,
sturdy, portable, and easy
to store. It's also simple to
make. Although the fold-
ing mechanism may look
complex, it doesn't require

any special joinery or
hardware. The rigid joints
are either doweled or
lapped, and the pivoting
joints are assembled with
bolts and metal straps. ●

Materials List

FINISHED DIMENSIONS

PARTS

A.	Long legs (2)	$^3/_4'' \times 5^3/_4'' \times 42^3/_4''$
B.	Short legs (2)	$^3/_4'' \times 1^3/_4'' \times 27''$
C.	Seat supports (2)	$^3/_4'' \times 1^3/_4'' \times 15^3/_4''$
D.	Seat brace	$^3/_4'' \times 1^3/_4'' \times 15^3/_8''$
E.	Seat slats (6)	$^3/_4'' \times 2^1/_4'' \times 42''$
F.	Long rails (3)	$^3/_4'' \times 1^3/_4'' \times 40^1/_2''$
G.	Short rails (2)	$^3/_4'' \times 1^3/_4'' \times 38^3/_4''$
H.	Straight splats (7)	$^3/_4'' \times 1^1/_2'' \times 14^3/_4''$
J.	Diamond splats (4)	$^3/_4'' \times 5^3/_4'' \times 14^3/_4''$
K.	Dowels (20)	$^3/_8''$ dia. $\times 2''$

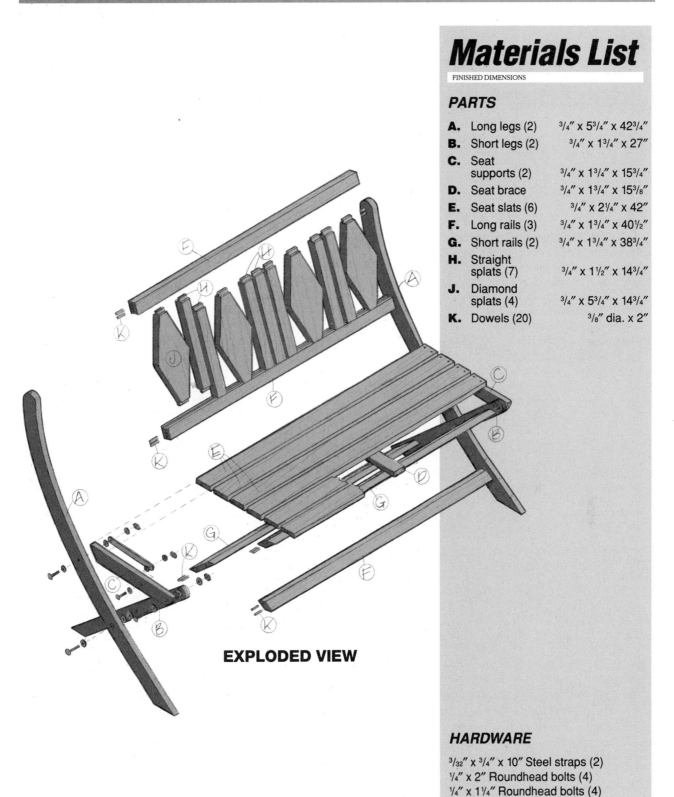

EXPLODED VIEW

HARDWARE

$^3/_{32}'' \times ^3/_4'' \times 10''$ Steel straps (2)
$^1/_4'' \times 2''$ Roundhead bolts (4)
$^1/_4'' \times 1^1/_4''$ Roundhead bolts (4)
$^1/_4''$ Stop nuts (8)
$^1/_4''$ Fender washers (12)
$^1/_4''$ Flat washers (16)
4d Galvanized finishing nails ($^1/_4$ lb.)

1
Select the stock and cut the parts to size. To make this project, you need about 18 board feet of 4/4 (four-quarters) stock. You can use almost any species of wood, as long as it's relatively clear and straight-grained. White pine, white cedar (called "juniper" in some areas), redwood, mahogany, and teak will stand up best to the weather. (The bench shown is made from white pine.) Avoid red cedar and pressure-treated wood. Red cedar is too soft and pressure treated wood is prone to splitting. While you can use them on some heavier pieces of outdoor furniture, the parts of this bench are too delicate.

After selecting the stock, plane it all to ³/₄″ thick. Cut the parts to the sizes given in the Materials List.

2
Cut the tenons and grooves. The back of the bench consists of splats and rails. These parts are joined with tenons and grooves, as shown in *Section A*. The splats have tenons on both ends, and rest in grooves in the edges of the rails.

Make the grooves first. Using a dado cutter or a table-mounted router, cut a ¹/₄″-wide, ³/₈″-deep groove in the bottom edge of the top back rail and the top edge of the bottom back rail. (See Figure 1.)

Cut the tenons to fit the grooves. Make a ³/₈″-wide, ¹/₄″-deep rabbet in the end of a ³/₄″ thick scrap, turn the scrap over, and cut a second rabbet in the same end. The two rabbets will form a ¹/₄″-thick, ³/₈″-long tenon. (See Figure 2.) Test the fit in the grooves. If the tenon is too loose, lower the bit or the cutter. If it's too tight, raise the bit or the cutter. When the tenon fits properly, cut tenons in the ends of all the splats.

1/Cut the grooves in the back rails with a dado cutter or a table-mounted router and a straight bit, as shown. If you use a router, make the grooves in several passes, cutting just ¹/₈″–¹/₄″ deeper with each pass.

2/To make the tenons, cut two matching rabbets in each end of each splat. Adjust the thickness of the tenon to fit the grooves in the rails.

3
Cut the shapes of the legs, seat supports, and diamond splats. Several of the bench parts are cut to a special shape — legs, supports, and splats. Since you must make at least two of each shape, pad saw and pad sand these parts — tape the stock together to make two or more parts at once. To make a pad, first wipe the wood with tack cloth to remove the sawdust. (This will ensure that the tape adheres properly — tape doesn't stick well to a dusty surface.) Stack the boards so the edges and ends are flush, and stick them together with double-faced carpet tape. (See Figure 3.)

3/To keep the stacks from shifting as you saw and sand them, stick them together with double-faced carpet tape.

Enlarge the *Long Leg Pattern* and trace it onto the top of the long leg stack. Lay out the seat supports (as shown in the *Seat Support Layout*) and short legs (as shown in the *Short Leg Layout*) on the top board of their respective stacks. Mark the shapes of the diamond splats, as shown in the *Front View,* on the top of the splat stack.

Cut all these shapes with a band saw or saber saw. (If you use a saber saw, you can only cut two duplicate parts at once — you'll have to make two stacks to cut the four diamond splats.) Sand the sawed edges smooth. Take the diamond splat stacks apart and discard the tape. However, do *not* take the leg or support stacks apart yet. Wait until after you drill the pivot holes.

4 **Make the metal pivot strap.** The pivoting mechanism for this bench includes two steel straps. These keep the seat in place as you fold the bench up or down. Using a hacksaw, cut these straps from $3/32$"-thick, $3/4$"-wide metal bar stock. (This is available in most hardware stores.) Round the ends, as shown in the *Pivot Strap Layout,* with a file or grinder.

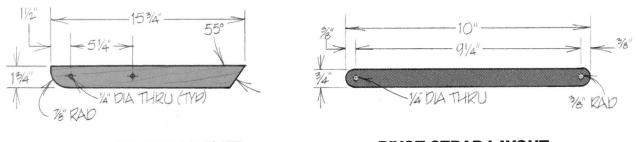

SEAT SUPPORT LAYOUT   **PIVOT STRAP LAYOUT**

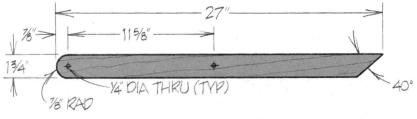

SHORT LEG LAYOUT

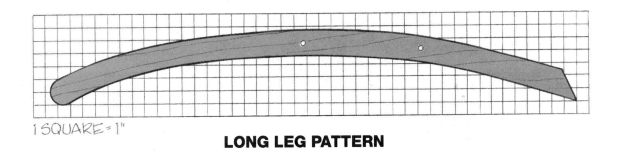

LONG LEG PATTERN

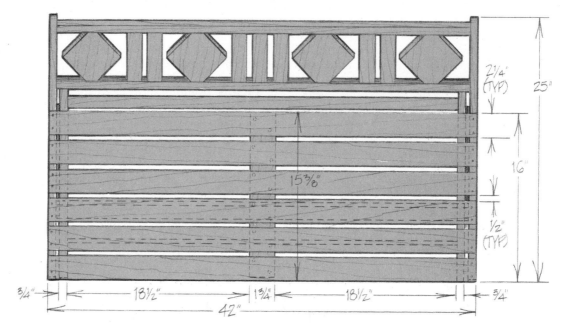

TOP VIEW

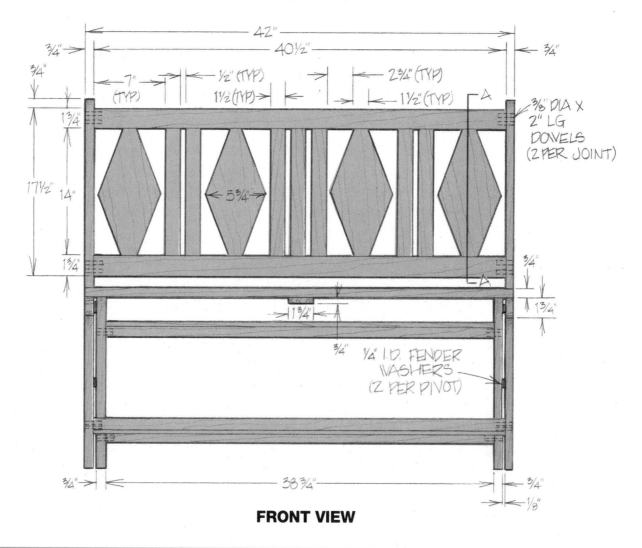

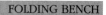

FRONT VIEW

5

Drill the pivot holes. Mark the location of the ¼″-diameter pivot holes on the top of the stacks of long legs, short legs, seat supports, and pivot straps. The locations of these holes are shown in the *Long Leg Layout, Short Leg Layout, Seat Support Layout,* and *Pivot Strap Layout.*

To find the pivot hole locations on the curved long legs, rest the stack on the workbench so the legs arch above it. Measure the locations of the holes along the surface of the bench, then transfer these measurements to the legs with a square. (See Figure 4.)

Drill the holes in the legs and supports with a ¼″-diameter wood bit. Take the stacks apart and discard the tape. Remove the wood bit from the drill and mount a high-speed steel bit. Bore the holes in the metal pivot straps.

4/To find the locations of the pivot holes in the curved long legs, rest the legs on the workbench with the curve up. Lay a tape measure or a straightedge flat on the workbench, under the leg. Transfer the measurements from the tape or stick to the leg stock with a square.

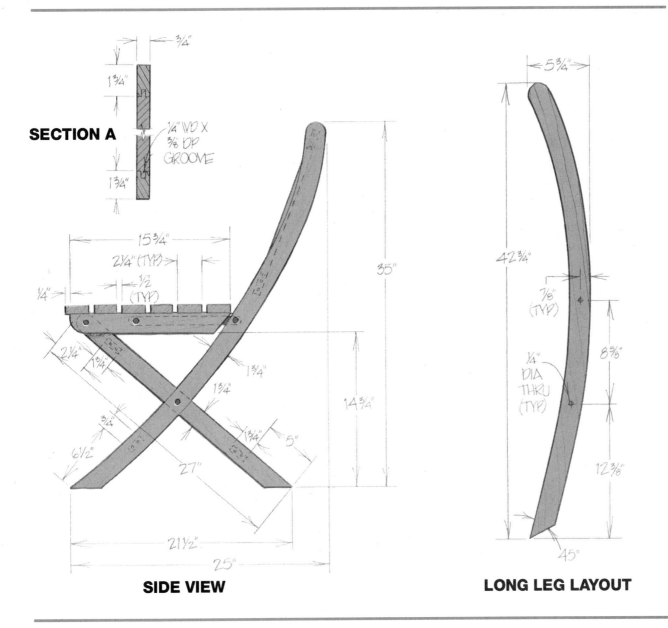

SIDE VIEW

LONG LEG LAYOUT

6

Assemble the bench. The assembled bench consists of three subassemblies — long leg assembly, short leg assembly, and seat assembly. Each of these is joined with bolts so it pivots on the others.

To begin assembly, finish sand all the parts. Using a doweling jig to guide the drill, make two $3/8''$-diameter, $1\frac{1}{2}''$-deep dowel holes in each end of each rail. The spacing of these holes isn't critical, but they should be approximately $1''$ apart.

Glue the tenoned ends of the splats into the grooves in the long rails. Arrange the splats as shown in the *Front View* to create the back. Since this project will be used outside, use a waterproof glue such as resorcinol or epoxy.

Mark the location of the rails on the long and short legs, as shown in the *Front View* and *Side View*. Place dowel centers in the holes in the rails, then press them against the legs where you want to join them. The dowel centers will leave small indentations. (See Figure 5.) Drill $3/8''$-diameter, $1/2''$-deep dowel holes at each of these indentations.

5/Use dowel centers to transfer the location of the dowel holes from the ends of the rails to the inside faces of the legs. When you place dowel centers in the rail holes and press the parts together, the centers will leave small indentations showing where to drill matching holes in the legs.

¼" STOP NUT
¼" FLAT WASHER
¼" FENDER WASHER
PIVOT STRAP
¼" FLAT WASHER
¼" X 1¼" R.H. BOLT
LONG LEG
SHORT LEG
¼" STOP NUT
¼" FLAT WASHER
¼" FENDER WASHERS
¼" FLAT WASHER
¼" X 2" R.H. BOLT

PIVOT ASSEMBLY DETAIL

Glue the legs and rails together, inserting dowels in the holes. Once again, use waterproof glue.

Lay the seat slats on the seat supports, spacing them as shown in the *Side View*. Attach the slats to the supports with 4d finishing nails, and set the heads of the nails. (Remember, the seat supports in the seat assembly must be *precisely* as far apart as the long legs in the long leg assembly.) To give the seat some added strength, nail the seat brace to the bottom surfaces of the seat slats. Once again, set the nails.

Bolt the short leg assembly *inside* the long leg assembly. To install each $\frac{1}{4}'' \times 2''$ roundhead bolt, first place a flat washer over the shaft. Insert the bolt through the appropriate pivot hole in the long leg, put two $\frac{1}{4}''$ fender washers over the bolt shaft, and insert it through the short leg. Place another flat washer over the shaft, then secure the bolt with a $\frac{1}{4}''$ stop nut, as shown in the *Pivot Assembly Detail*. This arrangement of bolts, washers, and nuts keeps the legs from rubbing and

reduces the wear and tear on the parts of the bench.

Bolt the seat assembly to the *outside* of the short leg assembly, just as you bolted the leg assemblies together. Then attach the pivot straps to the *insides* of the seat supports and the long leg assemblies with $\frac{1}{4}'' \times 1\frac{1}{4}''$ bolts — as you assembled the leg pivots, but use only one fender washer between the wooden parts and the metal strap.

Test the folding action. With the bench folded out, pull up on the back edge of the seat. The seat should lift up, then fold flat against the back. At the same time, the leg assemblies should come together like scissors. Fold the seat back down again. The legs should spread out and the mitered ends of the seat supports should rest against the curved edges of the long legs when the seat is horizontal. If the seat is angled forward when it's folded out, shave a little stock from the edges of the long legs where the supports touch. If it's angled back, glue shims to the mitered ends of the seat supports.

6/As the seat folds up, it pivots on the metal straps so the **back edge** raises.

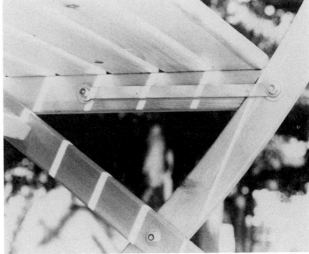

7/When folded down, the mitered ends of the supports rest against the long legs.

7 **Finish the bench.** Disassemble the bench into the three subassemblies — long leg assembly, short leg assembly, and seat. Remove all metal hardware. Do any necessary touch-up sanding, then apply at least two coats of an exterior finish to all wooden surfaces. When the finish dries, reassemble the bench.

Juggling Bench

This unusual bench first appeared in the southern American colonies in the early eighteenth century and quickly became a common sight on the porches of the region's plantations. Tradition has it that the bench was originally intended as a source of exercise for older men and women — they sat on the seat and lightly bounced up and down. The movement was pleasant and soothing, like swinging or rocking.

However, the bench soon became a source of mirth and entertainment for everyone, young and old alike. The design is wonderfully adaptable to your moods and physical condition. You can undulate up and down slowly and sedately, or jump like a kangaroo. Although the seat looks like it might break if you bend it too far, it is surprisingly resilient. When you get bouncing, the seat bends almost to the floor. And when it springs back, it can pitch you off if you don't hold on. Watching two or three rambunctious children play on the bench, you're reminded of a juggler tossing balls into the air — this may be how the bench got its name.

The juggling bench shown was built by Larry Heisey of Troy, Ohio, who copied it from an antique that he saw on the stately porch of a South Carolina plantation. He keeps it on his patio, where it serves as an icebreaker. "You'd be surprised at how many new friendships have started out bouncing up and down on this bench," he says.

Materials List

FINISHED DIMENSIONS

PARTS

A. Seat   1″ x 11¼″ x 120″

B. Supports (4)   1½″ x 3½″ x 24½″

C. Rockers (4)   1½″ x 3½″ x 17¾″

D. Stretchers (6)   1⅛″ dia. x 15⅛″

E. Keepers (4)   1⅛″ dia. x 6″

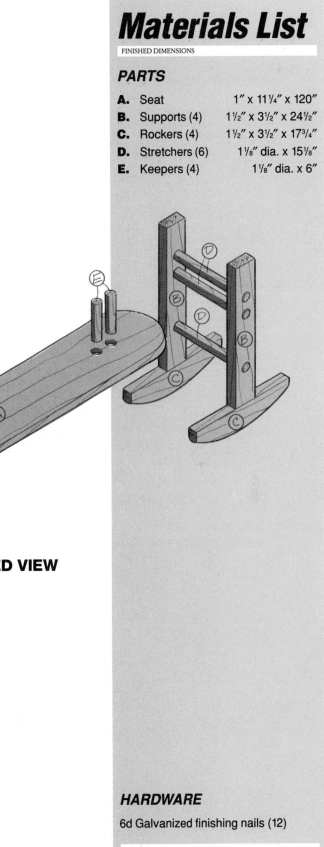

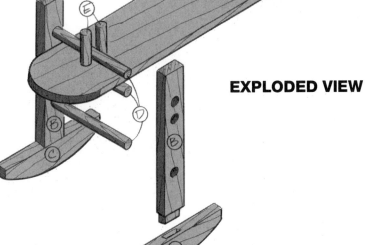

EXPLODED VIEW

HARDWARE

6d Galvanized finishing nails (12)

1 Select the stock and cut the parts to size.

To make this project, you need 10 board feet of 8/4 (eight-quarters) stock, 14 board feet of 5/4 (five-quarters), and a 10′ length of 1⅛″-diameter closet pole. Traditionally, these benches are made from pine or spruce — other woods are too brittle or quickly lose their bounce. Select clear stock for the seat if you can find it. Every knot weakens and reduces the resilience of a board. If you can't find perfectly clear stock, a few *solid* knots won't hurt.

After selecting the wood, plane the 8/4 stock to 1½″ thick, and the 5/4 stock to 1″ thick. Cut the parts to the sizes given in the Materials List.

2 Cut the mortises and tenons.

The supports and rockers are joined by mortises and tenons. Make the 1″-wide, 3″-long, 2″-deep mortises first — drill a series of overlapping 1″-diameter holes to remove most of the waste, then clean up the edges of the mortises with a chisel. (See Figures 1 and 2.) Make the tenons to fit the mortises. Using a dado cutter or a table-mounted router, cut a practice tenon in the end of a 1½″-thick, 3½″-wide scrap. (See Figure 3.) If the tenon is too large, raise the cutter or bit. If it's too small, lower it. When the practice tenon fits properly, cut tenons in the bottom ends of the supports.

1/Rough out each mortise on a drill press. Drill several overlapping 1″-diameter, 2″-deep holes to remove most of the waste.

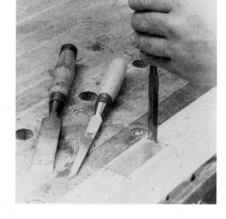

2/Remove the remaining waste and square the edges of the mortise with a chisel. A mortising chisel works best, if you have one.

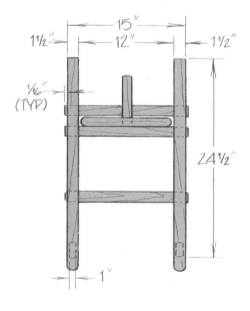

3/To make a tenon on the end of a support, cut a 2″-wide, ¼″-deep rabbet in one face of the board. Turn the board 90° and cut another rabbet in an edge. Repeat until you've cut both faces and both edges. The four rabbets will form a tenon.

END VIEW

3

Cut the shapes of the seat and rockers. Lay out the shapes of the seat and rockers, as shown in the *Top View* and *Side View*. Cut the shapes with a band saw, saber saw, or fretsaw, then sand the sawed edges.

> **TRY THIS!** To make four identical rockers, stack the boards and stick them together with double-faced carpet tape. Make sure that the ends and edges are flush, and that the mortises are all facing in the same direction. Saw and sand the shapes of the rockers with the parts stacked.

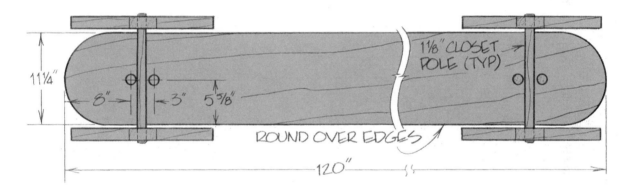

TOP VIEW

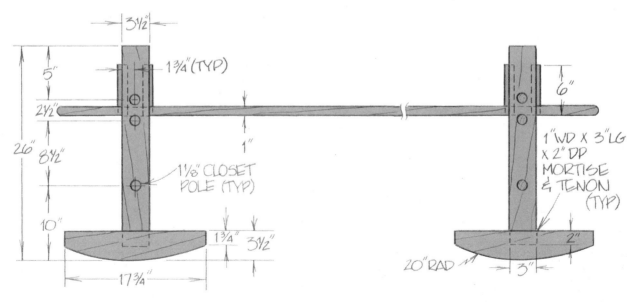

SIDE VIEW

4

Drill the holes needed in the supports and the seat. The stretchers fit into 1⅛″-diameter holes in the supports, and the keepers into 1⅛″-diameter holes in the seat. The fit must be snug, otherwise the bench may fall apart. Unfortunately, a closet pole, like all construction lumber, is not well dried and tends to shrink soon after it's cut. The pole you buy may not be quite 1⅛″ in diameter — it will likely be slightly smaller.

Drill a 1⅛″-diameter hole in a scrap and test the fit of one of the stretchers or keepers. If it's tight, lay out the locations of the holes on the seat and support, and drill them. If it's loose, there are two ways to solve the problem: (1) You can grind down the sides of a 1⅛″-diameter spade bit until it drills a hole precisely as large as the pole, or (2) you can turn 1″-diameter tenons on the ends of the round parts and drill 1″-diameter round mortises in the seat and supports. (See Figures 4 and 5.)

4/To grind a spade bit to drill a precise diameter, mark how much you want to remove. Use a tungsten carbide point to scratch the steel bit — the edge of an old router bit works well.

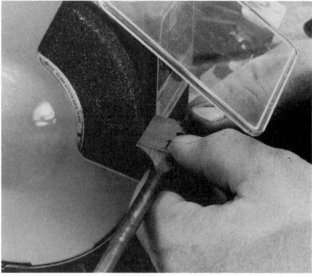

5/Then grind or file away the metal up to the marks. Remember, you must remove **precisely** as much steel on one side of the bit as you do on the other.

5

Assemble the bench. Finish sand all the parts. Round over the edges of the seat with a rasp and sandpaper. Also, sand a small chamfer on the ends of the stretchers.

Glue the tenoned ends of the supports into the mortised rockers. Since the bench may be left out in the weather, use a waterproof glue such as resorcinol or epoxy. Then glue the stretchers into the holes in the supports, making two separate support assemblies. Press the parts together until about ¹⁄₁₆″ of each

stretcher protrudes from the outside of each support, as shown in the *End View*. Reinforce each glue joint by driving a finishing nail through the edge of the support and into the stretcher. Set the heads of the nails.

Slide the seat into place between the top and middle stretchers of both support assemblies. Drive the keepers into the holes so they straddle the top stretchers. Do *not* glue them in place — the fit should be snug enough to hold them without glue. This will allow you to disassemble the bench when you need to store it or repair it.

6

Finish the bench. Remove the keepers and slide the seat free of the support assemblies. Do any necessary touch-up sanding, then apply an exterior finish to the completed bench. Traditionally, these benches were painted a dark, shiny green known as

Carolina green. If you can't find this color at a paint store, mix equal parts of green and black semi-gloss exterior paint to approximate the appearance of the traditional finish. When the finish dries, reassemble the bench.

Adirondack Settee and Stool

Few outdoor furniture styles have enjoyed the continued popularity of Adirondack furniture. It has remained a favorite for almost 100 years. Sit in an Adirondack chair or settee and you'll understand why. It is unusually relaxing — more like laying down than sitting. The flat, extra-wide arms provide surfaces to set a drink, a book, a portable radio, and other paraphernalia you might want.

Unlike some Adirondack furniture, the back and seat are curved to better fit your body. And if you really want to get comfortable, the matching stools give you a place to rest your legs.

All this comfort can be built easily and inexpensively from ordinary one-by and two-by construction lumber. There is no complex joinery — most of the parts are attached with wood screws. You can make a settee in a weekend, and have time left over to relax in it!

**SETTEE
EXPLODED VIEW**

Materials List

FINISHED DIMENSIONS

PARTS

Settee

A.	Front legs (2)	1½″ x 3½″ x 21½″
B.	Back legs (2)	1½″ x 5½″ x 36″
C.	Back braces (2)	1½″ x 3½″ x 26¼″
D.	Upper back support	1½″ x 5½″ x 42″
E.	Seat stretchers (2)	1½″ x 3½″ x 42″
F.	Seat brace	1½″ x 5½″ x 17¾″
G.	Leg stretcher	1½″ x 3½″ x 45″

H.	Lower back support	¾″ x 4¼″ x 46½″
J.	Back seat slat	¾″ x 4″ x 46½″
K.	Front seat slats (8)	¾″ x 1½″ x 46½″
L.	Back boards (13)	¾″ x 3½″ x 40½″
M.	Arm braces (2)	1½″ x 3″ x 7″
N.	Arms (2)	¾″ x 8″ x 31½″

Stool

A.	Front legs (2)	1½″ x 5½″ x 27¼″
B.	Back legs (2)	1½″ x 3½″ x 15¾″
C.	Stretchers (2)	1½″ x 3½″ x 18¾″
D.	Slats (13)	¾″ x 1½″ x 23¼″

**STOOL
EXPLODED VIEW**

HARDWARE

Settee

4d Galvanized finishing nails (¼ lb.)

#10 x 1¾" Flathead wood screws
(60–72)

#12 x 2½" Flathead wood screws
(20–24)

#12 x 3½" Flathead wood screws
(16–20)

Stool

4d Galvanized finishing nails (¼ lb.)

#10 x 1¾" Flathead wood screws
(26)

#12 x 2½" Flathead wood screws (8)

#12 x 3½" Flathead wood screws (8)

Making the Settee

1

Select the stock and cut the parts to size. To make the settee, you need two 8'-long 2 x 6s, three 8'-long 2 x 4s, and five 8'-long 1 x 12s. You can make this project from almost any wood, but if you plan to leave the settee outdoors, mahogany, teak, redwood, cypress, and cedar work best. These woods are naturally weather-resistant.

After selecting the stock, cut the parts to the sizes shown in the Materials List, except the *tapered* back boards. Cut eight of these boards ½"–¾" *wider* than shown. This will give you some cutting room when it comes time to make the tapers. The remaining five back boards are straight; cut these to the dimensions given.

Note: Although some of the back boards will eventually be trimmed considerably shorter than 40½", cut them all to this length initially. If the boards aren't all the same length when you make the taper cuts, the tapers won't match properly.

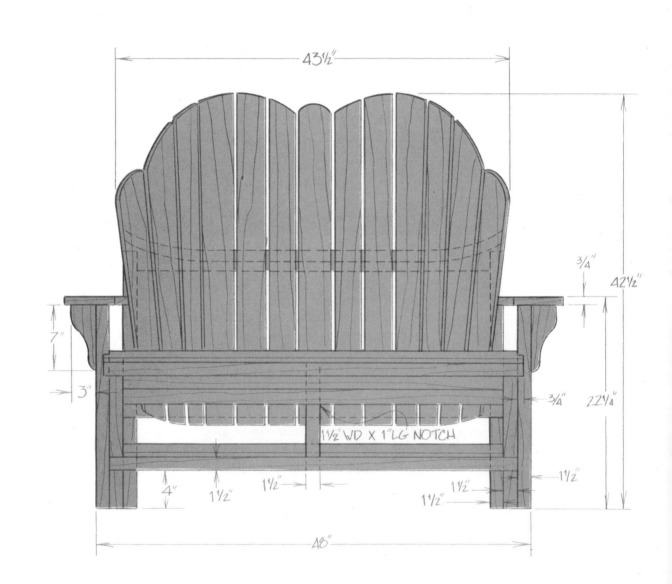

FRONT VIEW

You can also build this project from ordinary construction-grade lumber (either treated or untreated), but you must pick your boards carefully. Choose wood with as few splits and checks as possible. Stack the wood flat and let it dry for several months before using it. If you use untreated wood, coat all parts with a waterproof sealant as you put them together, then cover the completed project with an exterior finish. The settee shown was made of untreated yellow pine, and painted with exterior oil-base enamel.

2 **Cut the shapes of the settee parts.** Cut the miters needed. Miter the top ends of the back braces at 55° and the bottom ends of the back legs at 30°, as shown on the *Side View*.

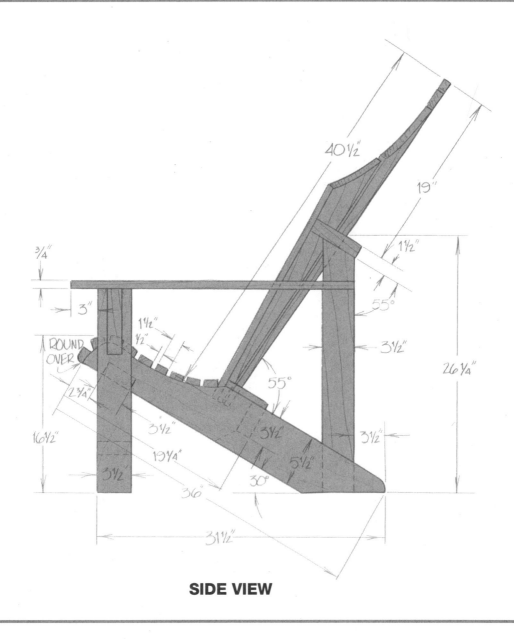

SIDE VIEW

Enlarge the *Arm, Arm Brace, Back Leg, and Seat Brace Patterns,* and trace these onto the stock. Also, lay out the upper back support, lower back support, and back seat slat, as shown in the *Upper Back Support* Layout and *Lower Back Support and Back Seat Slat Layouts.* Cut the shapes with a band saw or saber saw, and sand the sawed edges.

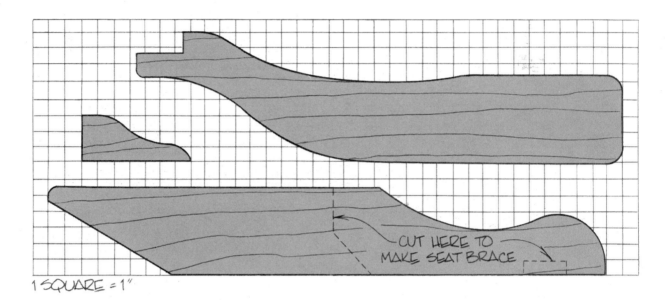

1 SQUARE = 1"

ARM, ARM BRACE, BACK LEG, AND SEAT BRACE PATTERNS

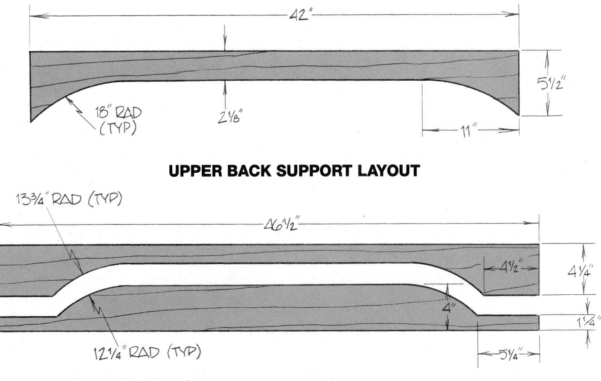

UPPER BACK SUPPORT LAYOUT

LOWER BACK SUPPORT AND BACK SEAT SLAT LAYOUTS

TRY THIS! You can scribe the arcs on the back supports and the back seat slat with a string compass, but you'll find it easier and more accurate to make yourself a compass stick. This is nothing more than a long, thin board — a wooden yardstick is ideal. Drill $\frac{1}{8}$"-diameter holes at $\frac{1}{4}$" intervals along the length of the board. To use this as a compass, put a finishing nail through one of the holes in the stick, and drive the nail into your workbench. Measure along the stick from the finishing nail to another hole and insert the sharp end of a pencil through the second hole. Then swing the arc.

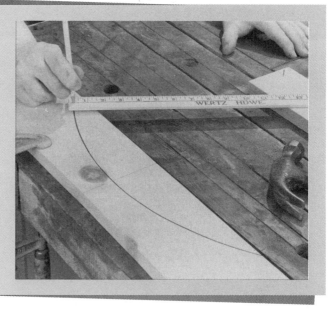

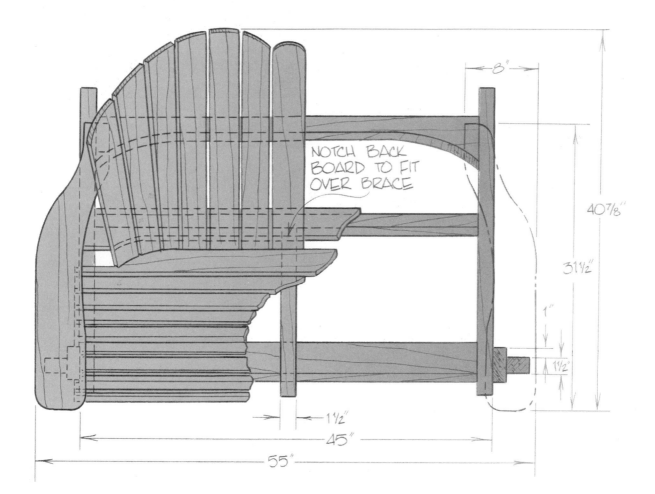

NOTCH BACK BOARD TO FIT OVER BRACE

8"

40⅞"

31½"

1"

1½"

1½"

45"

55"

TOP VIEW

3

Taper the back boards. While the five middle back boards are untapered, the four on either side (eight altogether) taper 1° from top to bottom. Of these, two are tapered on just one edge, and six (the three right-most and three left-most back boards) are tapered along both edges. To cut these tapers, make a tapering jig to hold the back boards 1° off parallel to the saw blade, as shown in the *Tapering Jig Layout*. Place the jig on the table saw, against the fence, and place a back board in the jig. Adjust the position of the fence so the blade will begin cutting near the top corner of the back board. Cut a taper in one edge of eight back boards. (See Figure 1.) The boards should taper from 3½″ wide at the top end to 2¾″ wide at the bottom.

Save the scrap from the first set of taper cuts. Place one of these scraps in the jig to serve as a spacer for the second set. Butt the tapered edge of a back board against the scrap and taper-cut the opposite side. (See Figure 2.) Repeat until you have tapered both edges of six back boards. These should taper from 3½″ wide at the top end to 2″ wide at the bottom.

*1/From a scrap of ¾″ plywood, make a jig to cut a 1° taper in the back boards. Cut a taper in **one** edge of **eight** back boards.*

2/From the eight back boards that you just tapered, select six to taper both edges. Place a scrap from the first set of taper cuts in the taper jig, butt the tapered edge of each board against this scrap, and cut the second taper.

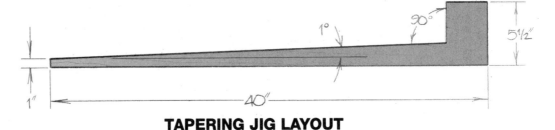

TAPERING JIG LAYOUT

4

Finish sand the parts. Sand the unassembled parts of the settee to remove any snags or other irregularities in the wood. If you're working with untreated pine, coat the wood with a waterproof sealant. Apply two coats to the bottoms of the legs. If you plan to paint the completed settee, apply the first coat before you assemble the parts.

5

Assemble the frame. Position the front legs and the back supports on the back legs. Make sure that the front legs and the supports are parallel. When they're properly placed, mark their positions. Fasten them to the back leg with #12 x 2½″ flathead wood screws. Remember that the two leg assemblies should be mirror images of each other.

Fasten the arm braces and arms in place, using the same size screws. Countersink all the screws, so the heads are flush with the surface of the wood. If you want to hide the screw heads completely, counterbore and countersink the screws. Later, you can cover the heads with wooden plugs.

Tie the leg-and-arm assemblies together with the stretchers and back supports. Use #12 x 3½″ screws to attach the upper back support and the stretchers. Toe-nail the front seat stretcher, driving the screws through the stretcher edges at an angle and into the back legs. Attach the lower back support with #10 x 1¾″ screws.

Measure and mark the middle of the seat stretchers. Attach the seat brace to the seat stretcher at these points, using #12 x 2½″ screws.

TRY THIS!   You'll find that this project, when assembled, is too large to fit through a door less than 32″ wide. To save yourself from a potential headache, assemble the settee outside or in your garage.

6 Attach the back boards to the chair.
Temporarily tack the back boards to the frame. Start with the middle board — cut a 1½″-wide, 1″-long notch in the bottom end, as shown in the *Front View,* so it fits over the seat brace. Tack it to the frame, then tack other boards to the right and left, spacing them ⅜″–½″ apart.

Space the five straight back boards along the middle of the frame. Then tack the boards with a single taper to the right and left of the straight back boards — the tapered edges must face the outside. Finally, add the double-tapered back boards, filling out the frame. Use finishing nails (so you don't make large holes), and don't drive them all the way home (so you can pull them out again). Try to space the boards as evenly as possible. If they don't appear evenly spaced, remove the nails and rearrange the boards. When all the boards are properly positioned, replace the finishing nails one at a time with #10 x 1¾″ screws.

7 Attach the seat slats.
Temporarily nail the seat slats in place, just as you did with the back boards. Tack them down with finishing nails so you can easily readjust their positions if necessary. Several of the slats will have to be shortened to 45″ or notched to fit around the legs. (See Figure 3.) When all the slats are in position, remove the nails and replace them with screws.

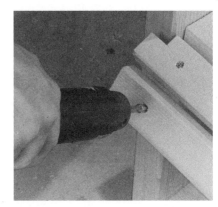

3/When positioning the seat slats, you'll have to cut a few of them short or notch them to fit around the legs.

8 Cut the shape of the back.
After the back boards and seat slats are securely fastened to the frame, lay out the shape of the back, as shown in the *Back Board Layout,* on the front surface of the backboards. Lay the settee across blocks or sawhorses so the back is horizontal, with the front surface facing up. Cut the top ends of the back boards with a saber saw, then sand the sawed ends. (See Figure 4.)

*4/Cut the shape of the back with a saber saw **after** you've fastened the back boards securely to the settee frame.*

9

Finish the settee. Using a block plane, round over the front-most corner of the front seat slat (see Figure 5) to prevent it from pressing against the backs of your (or someone else's) legs. Round over all the other hard edges with a rasp and sander to "soften" them. Do any necessary touch-up sanding on the flat surface.

If you're painting or finishing the settee, apply a second coat now. (You should have applied the first one before you assembled the parts.) Apply a little extra to the top ends of the back boards, where you cut the shape of the back. If you've built this project from a weather-resistant wood, there's no need to apply a finish. The natural oils or pressure-applied chemicals keep it from rotting.

5/Round over the front-most corner of the front seat slat with a plane. Otherwise, the hard, square corner may bite into the backs of sitters' legs.

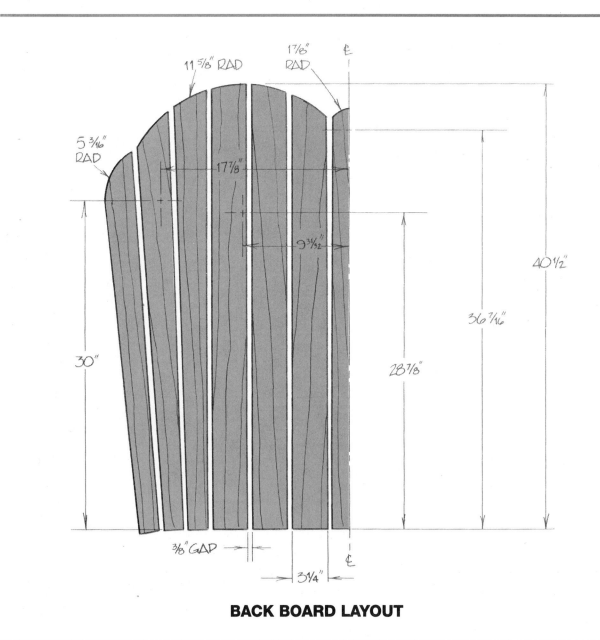

BACK BOARD LAYOUT

Making the Stools

10

Cut the parts to size. To make two stools, you need the leftover lumber from the settee, plus one 8'-long 2 x 6, one 8'-long 2 x 4, and one 8'- long 2 x 12. Cut the parts to the sizes given in the Materials List.

11

Cut the shapes of the legs. Miter the top ends of the back legs at 15°, and the bottom ends of the back legs at 43°. Stack the parts so you can cut both front legs and both back legs at the same time. Enlarge the *Front Leg Pattern* and trace it onto the top board in the front leg stack. Lay out the back leg as shown in the *Back Leg Layout* on the top board of the back leg stack. Cut the shapes with a band saw or fretsaw, and sand the sawed edges smooth. Take the stacks apart and discard the tape.

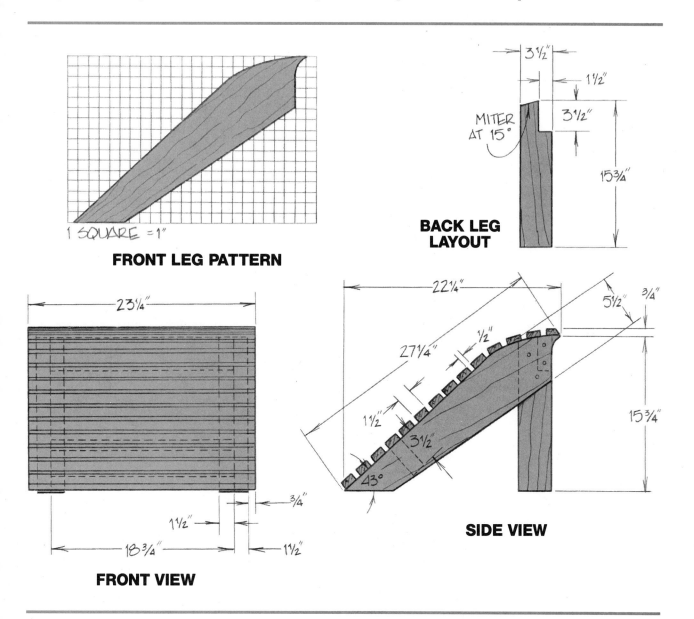

1 SQUARE = 1"

FRONT LEG PATTERN

BACK LEG LAYOUT

FRONT VIEW

SIDE VIEW

12

Finish sand the parts. Sand the unassembled parts to remove any snags or other irregularities. If you're working with untreated lumber, coat the wood with a waterproof sealant. Apply two coats to the bottoms of the legs. If you plan to paint the stools, apply the first coat before you assemble the parts.

13

Assemble the stools. Attach the back legs to the front legs with #12 x 2½″ flathead wood screws, countersinking the heads. Join the leg assemblies by driving #12 x 3½″ screws through the front leg and into the ends of the stretchers. Also, drive #12 x 2½″ screws through the back stretcher and into the front legs. Clamp the parts to keep them from shifting while you drive the screws.

Temporarily tack the slats in place with finishing nails so you can easily readjust their positions, if necessary. Then remove the nails and replace them with #10 x 1¾″ screws.

14

Finish the stools. Using a block plane, round over the back corner of the back slat. Round over all the other hard edges with a rasp and sander, and do any necessary touch-up sanding. If necessary, apply a finish to match the settee.

Re-Drying Wood

You may be tempted to build your outdoor benches and swings from construction-grade lumber for two reasons. First, it saves money — construction-grade lumber is a fraction of the cost of cabinet-grade. Second, some construction-grade lumber weathers well. Construction redwood, cedar, and cypress all have natural oils that make them resistant to rot and mildew. Pressure-treated lumber — wood that has been impregnated with chromated copper arsenate (CCA) — is widely available, inexpensive, and almost impervious to the weather. By picking through a lumberyard's piles looking for straight boards with solid knots and no checks, you can usually find wood that's good enough for furniture.

Unfortunately, even though it may look good enough, it's probably not — yet. Construction-grade lumber is only dried to 19 percent moisture content, even though it may be stamped "kiln-dried." Wood just begins to shrink and distort when it drops below 25 percent moisture content, and doesn't become stable enough for furnituremaking until it's below 10 percent. If you make a bench or a swing from construction-grade lumber straight out of the lumberyard, the wood may change shape *as you work with it.* You may cut the parts of a project one weekend, then attempt to assemble them the next and find they've warped or twisted. Even if you cut and assemble the parts in one day, your project may be ruined as the boards dry out. They may crack, split, or pull apart as the wood shrinks.

To prevent this, you must "re-dry" the wood before you use it. Purchase about 20 percent more wood than you think you'll need. This will give you extra stock in case some of the boards warp or split as they dry. Store the wood in a protected, out-of-the-way, *well-ventilated* location — garage, shed, basement, or crawl space. Don't put it in a completely closed area, or where heat might build up. Poor ventilation will prevent the wood from drying, and excessive heat will cause it to dry too fast. (If wood dries too fast, it may check or split.) (See Figure A.)

Stack the wood *horizontally.* Arrange each layer so it's as wide as the layer beneath it. That way, each layer will be properly supported and the weight of the wood from above and below will help keep the boards straight and flat as they dry. Leave a gap between the edges of each board to let the air circulate. If you position them too close, the boards on the inside of the stack will not dry properly. (See Figure B.)

Space the boards vertically with "stickers" — long, slender strips of wood. Place the stickers directly

(Continued)

Re-Drying Wood — Continued

over one another, as shown in Figure C. This will keep the boards from bowing.

When you've stacked the boards, seal the end grain with an exterior paint. (See Figure D.) Water evaporates from the ends of the boards more rapidly than the faces or edges. If the ends are left untreated, the boards will shrink faster at the ends than in the middle, and the wood will split or check.

Let the wood sit for several months before using it. You won't have to dry the wood as long as you might dry green lumber, since it has already been partially kiln-dried. Nor do you have to get it as dry

as cabinet-grade lumber. The joinery in outdoor furniture should allow for more wood movement than you'd expect to find in indoor furniture.

To tell whether the wood is dry enough to use, take a piece from the inside of the stack. Make a test cut and rub the sawdust between your fingers. If the dust feels moist, the wood needs to sit longer. If you can feel no moisture, it's ready to use. Experienced woodworkers can also tell if a board is dry by tapping it with a hammer. On a wet board, the tap will sound dull and indistinct. A dry board has a ring to it — the tap is sharp and has a definite tone.

A/If the moisture is removed from a board too quickly, it will form surface checks. This is sometimes called "case hardening."

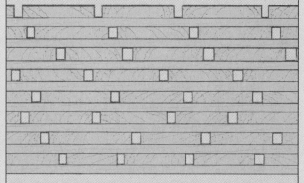

B/When you stack the lumber to re-dry it, leave gaps between the edges of the boards. Stagger the boards so no two edge-gaps are directly above or below one another. This will help to circulate the air throughout the stack.

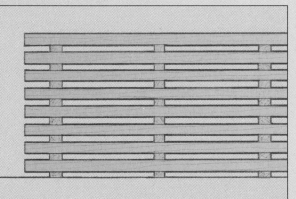

C/Although you must stagger the gaps, the stickers must be placed directly above and below one another. This properly supports the pile, and prevents the boards from drying with a bend or bow.

D/Paint the ends of the boards to prevent them from checking. If left unpainted, the ends will dry out faster than the rest of the board.

Garden Settle

An old-time "settle" was often a combination of a bench and a chest. Since space in many early American homes was at a premium, furniture often did double duty. A settle provided both seating and storage.

This garden settle does the same. The seat also serves as the lid to a box, in which you can store small hand tools, potting materials, hose, sprinklers, and other gardening items. And when you're done working in your garden, you can rest a while on the settle, surveying your handiwork.

The only difference between this settle and a traditional version is that this one is designed to be used outside. The joinery is very simple, the wood is weather-resistant, and the interior of the chest is well ventilated so moisture won't collect inside.

Materials List

FINISHED DIMENSIONS

PARTS

A.	Sides (2)	1½" x 16" x 34"
B.	Side cleats (4)	¾" x ¾" x 16"
C.	Front/back planks (4)	¾" x 7" x 32"
D.	Bottom planks (2)	¾" x 7⅞" x 29"
E.	Top	¾" x 3¾" x 32"
F.	Seat	¾" x 14¾" x 40"
G.	Long seat braces (2)	¾" x 1½" x 13¾"
H.	Short seat braces (2)	¾" x 1½" x 12"
J.	Backrest	¾" x 4" x 40"

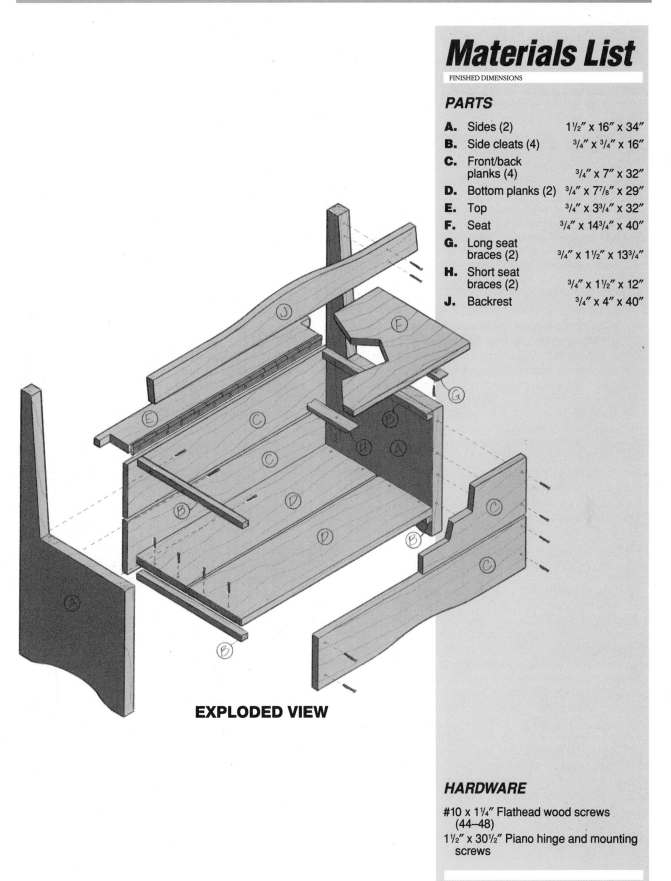

EXPLODED VIEW

HARDWARE

#10 x 1¼" Flathead wood screws (44–48)

1½" x 30½" Piano hinge and mounting screws

1

Select the stock and cut the parts to size. To make this project, you need about 16 board feet of 8/4 (eight-quarters) stock, and 18 board feet of 4/4 (four-quarters) stock. If you will keep this settle in a protected location, you can build it from almost any wood. However, if you plan to leave it outdoors, make it from mahogany, teak, redwood, cypress, or cedar — all these woods have natural oils that help them to withstand the weather. The settle shown is made from cedar.

You can also use pressure-treated lumber — white or yellow pine that has been impregnated with chemicals to make it weather-resistant. Pressure-treated wood, however, only comes in construction grades and is not well dried. Carefully pick through the piles at the lumberyard to find wood with as few defects as possible. After you bring it home, stack it flat in a protected area. Put spacers between the boards so that air can circulate around all surfaces, then let the wood dry for several months before using it.

After selecting and preparing the wood, glue up stock to make the widths you need for the sides and seat. If the project will be used outside, use a waterproof glue such as resorcinol or epoxy. Then cut all the parts to the sizes given in the Materials List.

2

Cut the shapes of the sides, top, backrest, and lower front/back planks.
Several of the parts on this settle are cut to shape — the sides, top, backrest, lower front plank, and lower back plank. Lay out the sides as shown in the *Side Layout,* and the top as shown in the *Top Layout.* Enlarge the *Front/Back Plank Pattern* and *Backrest Pattern* and trace them onto the stock. Cut the shapes with a band saw, fretsaw, or saber saw, then sand the sawed edges.

Warning: If you're sanding pressure-treated lumber, be sure to wear a dust mask — because of the chemical used to treat the wood, the sawdust is toxic. The dust from teak and cedar is also mildly toxic.

TRY THIS! Since the sides are precisely the same, you can save time by cutting them both at once. Stack the parts so the edges and ends are flush, then fasten them together with double-faced carpet tape. Lay out the shapes on the top part and cut the stack. Sand the sawed edges while the parts are still together, then take the stack apart and discard the tape. You can also use this procedure to shape the lower planks.

3

Assemble the settle. If you plan to apply a paint, stain, or varnish, finish sand the parts. If not, lightly sand all surfaces to clean up the wood. Fasten the cleats to the sides with screws. Drill oversize pilot holes for these screws — this will allow the sides to expand and contract with changes in the weather.

Note: Countersink all screws on the *inside* and *bottom* of the bench (where they can't be seen), so the heads are flush with the surface of the wood. Counterbore *and* countersink the screws on the *outside;* later, you can hide these screw heads with wooden plugs.

Fasten the front, back, and bottom planks to the sides and cleats. Leave a ¼" gap between these planks, as shown on the *Side View* and *Top View.* These gaps serve two important purposes. They let the planks move and they help ventilate the storage space. When the planks are secure, fasten the top and the backrest in place.

TRY THIS! Instead of using screws and covering the heads, use galvanized 8d decking nails and let the heads show. This will give a rustic look to the bench.

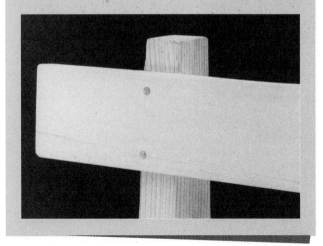

4 **Attach the seat.** Lay the seat in place and mark the positions of the long seat braces — there should be a $1/16''$ gap between the sides and the braces. Also, mark the mortise for the piano hinge. Remove the seat and mark the positions of the short seat braces.

Cut the mortise in the lid with a band saw or a fret- saw. Round the ends of the long braces with a band saw and a sander, as shown in the *Side View*. Attach both the long and short seat braces to the lid with wood screws. As you did when attaching the cleats to the sides, drill oversize pilot holes in the braces. This will let the lid expand and contract. With the braces in place, attach the lid to the top with a piano hinge.

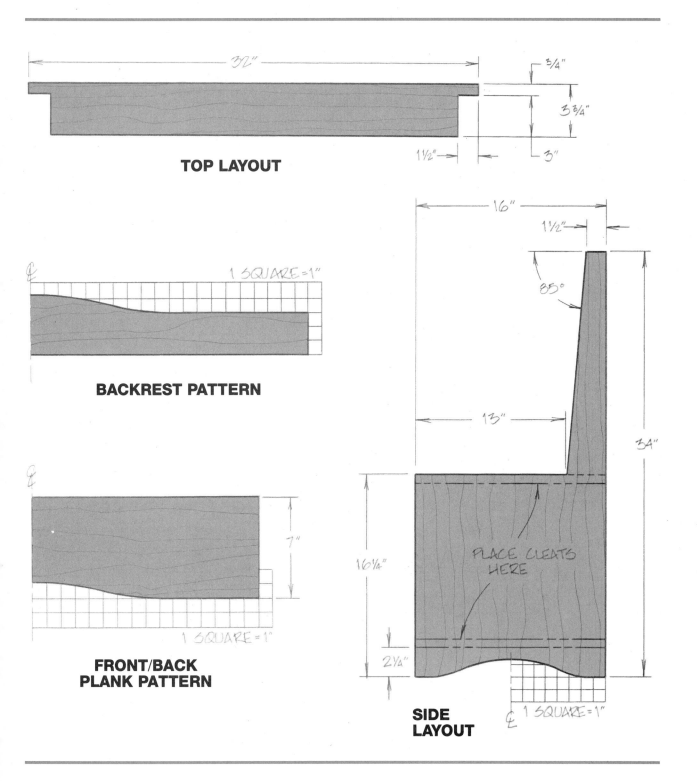

TOP LAYOUT

BACKREST PATTERN

FRONT/BACK PLANK PATTERN

SIDE LAYOUT

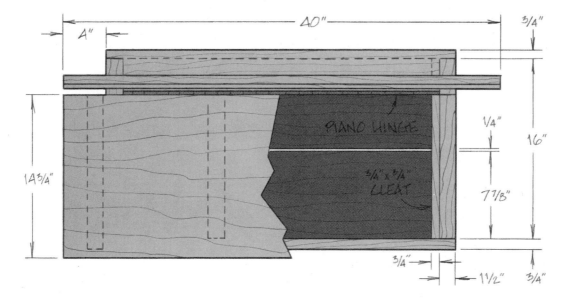

TOP VIEW

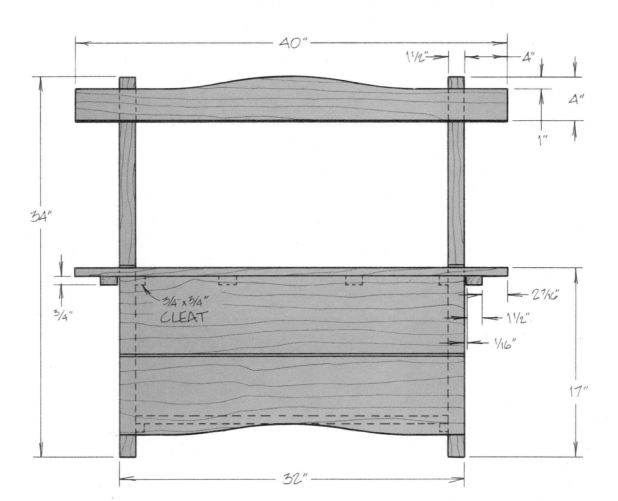

FRONT VIEW

5

Finish the settle. Install wooden plugs in the counterbores, gluing them in place with waterproof resorcinol or epoxy. When the glue dries, sand the plugs flush with the surface of the wood. (See Figures 1 through 4.)

Using a rasp and a sander, round over all the hard edges and corners on the assembled settle. This will make it more comfortable to sit on. If you plan to apply paint or another finish, remove the lid and the hinges. Do any necessary touch-up sanding, then finish the settle. Coat both the inside *and* outside of the project — this will help keep the wood from warping or twisting. When the finish dries, reattach the lid.

1/To cover the screw heads with wooden plugs, first select a ¾"-wide scrap of wood from the same stock you used to build the project. Using a plug cutter, bore ½"-long plugs, making several extra.

2/Since the plugs aren't as long as the wood is thick, they will remain attached to the scrap. Split them off by resawing the scrap with a band saw or fretsaw.

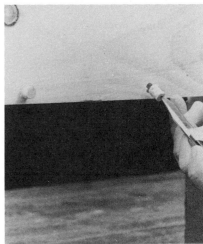

3/To cover a screw head, dip one end of a plug in glue and insert it in the counterbore. Make sure that the grain of the plug runs the same direction as the wood grain. Tap the plug all the way into the counterbore.

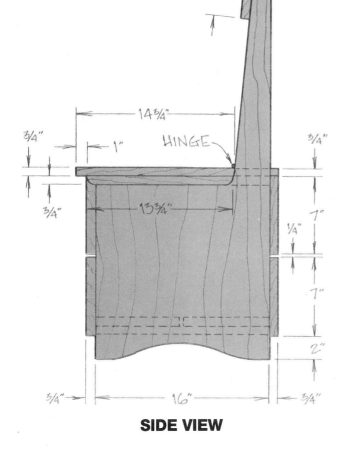

SIDE VIEW

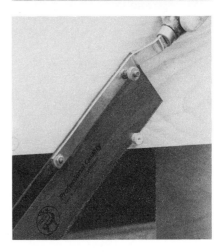

4/When the glue dries, cut the plugs off about 1/16" above the surface with a dovetail saw. Then sand the plugs flush with the surface.

Lawn Glider

A lawn glider appeals to the Rube Goldberg in all of us, that part of our character that loves a contraption. It's little more than a collection of sticks, bolted together at odd angles. But when you set it swinging and all the sticks move together, it's poetry in motion. You'll find that a lawn glider is as fascinating and relaxing to watch as it is to sit in.

This particular glider offers several additional features. It holds four people and seats them so they face one another, making the glider a pleasant place to hold a conversation. It supports a sunshade which moves in unison with the other moving parts, helping to keep everyone cool. And it's collapsible. By loosening just four bolts, you can take the glider apart, fold it flat, and store it for the winter.

It can be built in two different sizes. The lawn glider shown is made for children, and you can also build an adult-size version.

**FRAME
EXPLODED VIEW**

Materials List

PARTS

Frame (Child Size)

A.	Legs (4)	$^3/_4''$ x $1^3/_4''$ x 63''
B.	Top frame stretchers (2)	$^3/_4''$ x $1^3/_4''$ x 28''
C.	Bottom frame stretchers (2)	$^3/_4''$ x $1^3/_4''$ x $44^5/_8''$
D.	Leg braces (4)	$^3/_4''$ x $1^3/_4''$ x $20^1/_4''$
E.	Top frame stiffeners (2)	$^3/_4''$ x $1^3/_4''$ x $31^1/_4''$
F.	Bottom frame stiffeners (2)	$^3/_4''$ x $1^3/_4''$ x $47^3/_4''$
G.	Cross ties (4)	$^3/_4''$ x $1^3/_4''$ x $32^1/_4''$
H.	Spacers (2)	$1^3/_4''$ dia. x $^3/_4''$

Frame (Adult Size)

A.	Legs (4)	$1^1/_2''$ x $3^1/_2''$ x $100^3/_4''$
B.	Top frame stretchers (2)	$1^1/_2''$ x $3^1/_2''$ x 45''
C.	Bottom frame stretchers (2)	$1^1/_2''$ x $3^1/_2''$ x $71^1/_2''$
D.	Leg braces (4)	$1^1/_2''$ x $3^1/_2''$ x $32^3/_8''$
E.	Top frame stiffeners (2)	$1^1/_2''$ x $3^1/_2''$ x $50^1/_8''$
F.	Bottom frame stiffeners (2)	$1^1/_2''$ x $3^1/_2''$ x $76^1/_2''$
G.	Cross ties (4)	$1^1/_2''$ x $3^1/_2''$ x $51^5/_8''$
H.	Spacers (2)	$3^1/_2''$ dia. x $1^1/_2''$

(Continued)

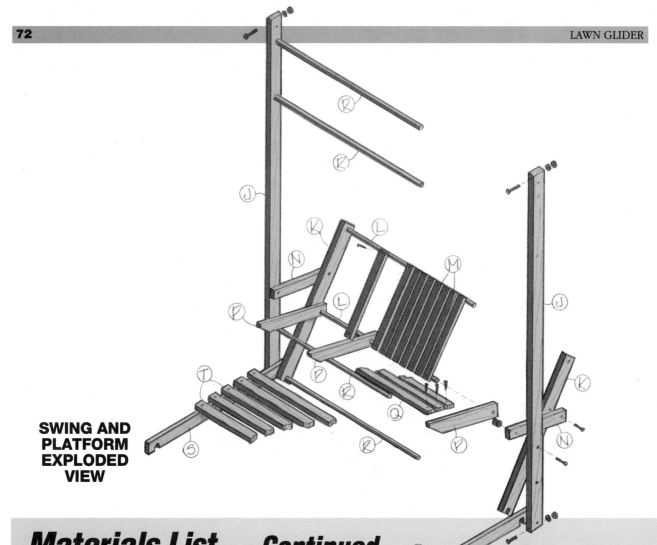

**SWING AND
PLATFORM
EXPLODED
VIEW**

Materials List — Continued

FINISHED DIMENSIONS

PARTS

Swings and Platform (Child Size)

J. Swing
supports (4) $3/4''$ x $1^3/4''$ x $52''$

K. Back
supports (4) $3/4''$ x $1^3/4''$ x $26^3/4''$

L. Back stretchers (4) $3/4''$ dia. x $25''$

M. Back splats (32) $3/8''$ x $7/8''$ x $15''$

N. Arms (4) $3/4''$ x $1^3/4''$ x $10^1/2''$

P. Seat supports (6) $3/4''$ x $1^3/4''$ x $9''$

Q. Seat slats (12) $3/8''$ x $7/8''$ x $24''$

R. Platform
stretchers (8) $3/4''$ dia. x $28''$

S. Platform
supports (2) $3/4''$ x $1^3/4''$ x $24''$

T. Platform slats (7) $3/4''$ x $1^1/2''$ x $28''$

Swings and Platform (Adult Size)

J. Swing
supports (4) $1^1/2''$ x $3^1/2''$ x $83^1/4''$

K. Back
supports (4) $1^1/2''$ x $3^1/2''$ x $42^7/8''$

L. Back
stretchers (4) $1^1/4''$ dia. x $39''$

M. Back
splats (32) $3/4''$ x $1^5/16''$ x $24''$

N. Arms (4) $1^1/2''$ x $3^1/2''$ x $16^7/8''$

P. Seat
supports (6) $1^1/2''$ x $3^1/2''$ x $14^3/8''$

Q. Seat slats (12) $3/4''$ x $1^5/16''$ x $37''$

R. Platform
stretchers (8) $1^1/4''$ dia. x $45''$

S. Platform
supports $1^1/2''$ x $3^1/2''$ x $38^3/8''$

T. Platform slats (7) $1^1/2''$ x $3''$ x $45''$

Sunshade (Child Size)

U. Sunshade
supports (2) $3/4''$ x $1^3/4''$ x $56''$

V. Sunshade
trusses (4) $3/4''$ x $6^1/8''$ x $25''$

W. Sunshade
slats (12) $3/8''$ x $2''$ x $58''$

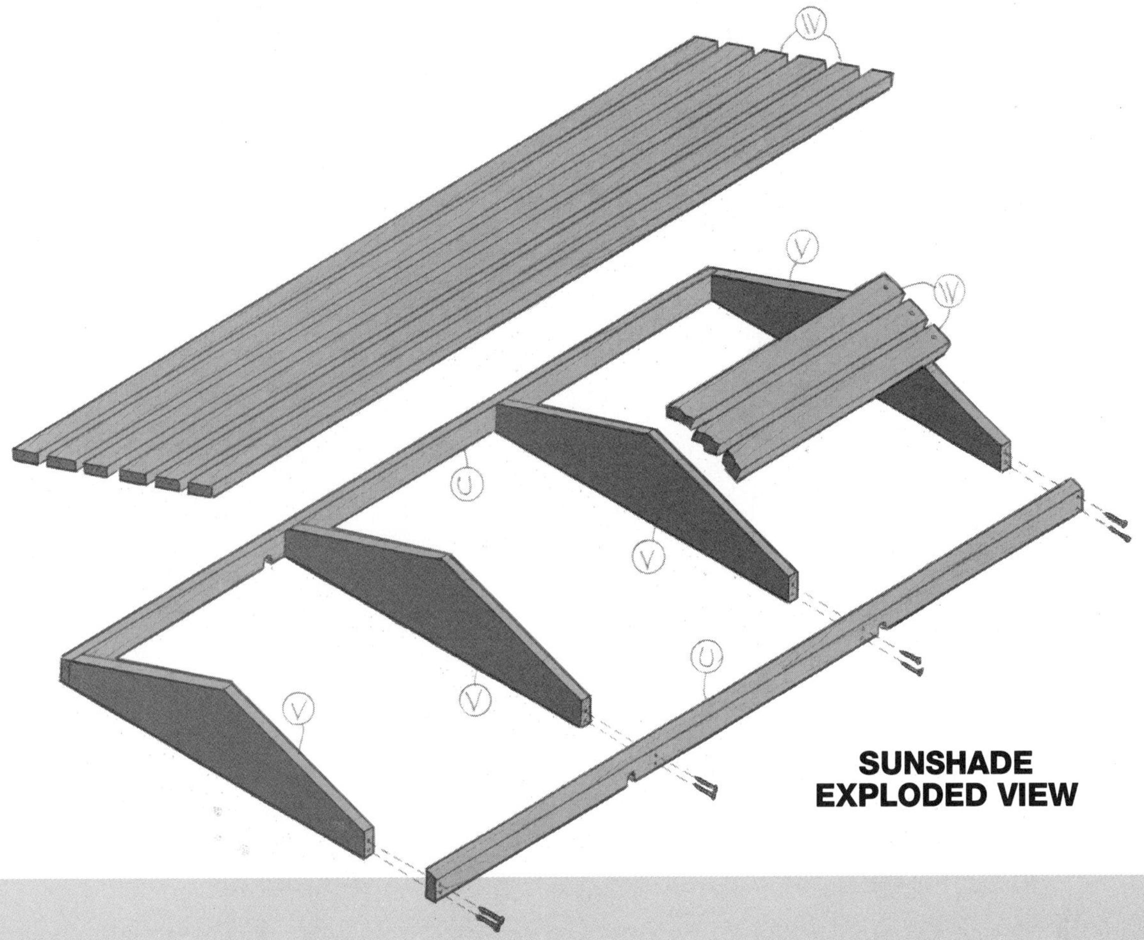

**SUNSHADE
EXPLODED VIEW**

HARDWARE

Sunshade (Adult Size)

U. Sunshade
supports (2) 1½" x 3½" x 89⅝"

V. Sunshade
trusses (4) ¾" x 9½" x 39"

W. Sunshade
slats (12) ¾" x 3⅛" x 92⅝"

Glider (Child Size)

⅜" dia. x 34½" Metal rods (2)
⅜" Flat washers (4)
⅜" Stop nuts (4)
¼" x 2" Hex bolts (14)
¼" x 2" Carriage bolts (8)
¼" Flat washers (66)
¼" Stop nuts (10)
¼" Wing nuts (4)
¼" Hex nuts (8)
2½"" Cotter pins (4)
4d Galvanized finishing nails (¼ lb.)
8d Galvanized spiral decking nails
(½ lb.)

Glider (Adult Size)

¾" O.D. x 55⅛" Pipe, threaded both
ends (2)
¾" Flat washers (4)
¾" Pipe nuts (4)
⅜" x 3½" Carriage bolts (14)
⅜" Flat washers (24)
⅜" Stop nuts (10)
⅜" Wing nuts (4)
¼" x 4" Carriage bolts (12)
¼" Flat washers (12)
¼" Hex nuts (8)
¼" Wing nuts (4)
6d Galvanized finishing nails (½ lb.)
12d Galvanized spiral decking nails
(¼ lb.)
16d Galvanized spiral decking nails
(1 lb.)

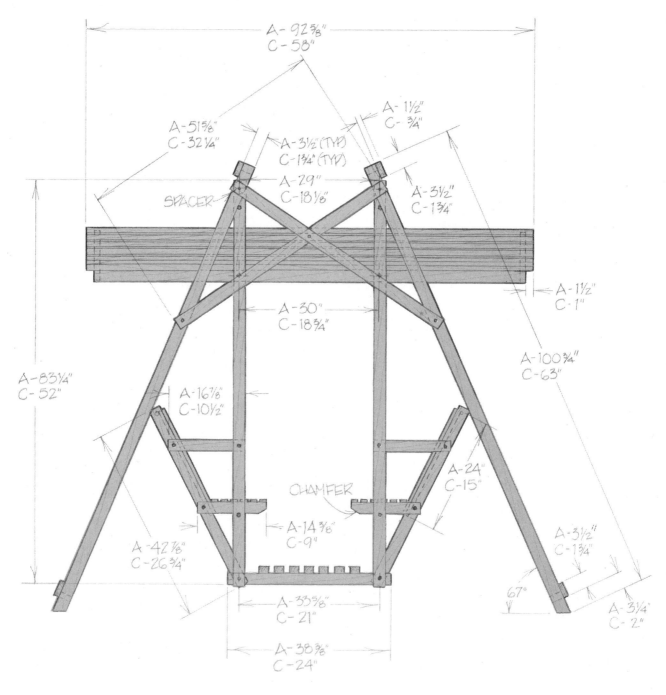

A- 92⅝"
C- 58"

A- 1½"
C- ¾"

A-51⅝"
C- 32¼"

A-3½" (TYP)
C-1¾" (TYP)

A- 29"
C-18⅛"

A-3½"
C-1¾"

SPACER

A- 1½"
C- 1"

A- 30"
C-18¾"

A-83¼"
C- 52"

A-100¾"
C-63"

A-16⅞"
C-10½"

A-24"
C-15"

CHAMFER

A-3½"
C-1¾"

A-14⅜"
C-9"

A -42⅞"
C-26¾"

67°

A- 3¼"
C- 2"

A-33⅝"
C- 21"

A-38⅜"
C-24"

SIDE VIEW

A–ADULT SIZE
C–CHILD SIZE

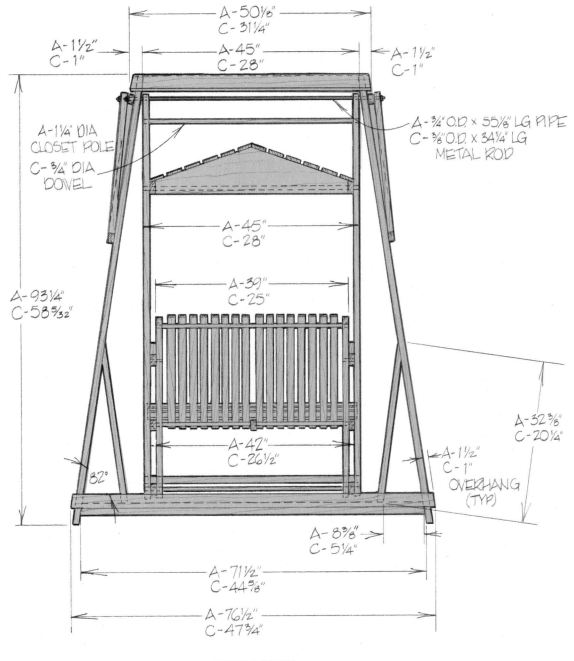

A—50⅛"
C—31¼"

A—1½"
C—1"

A—45"
C—28"

A—1½"
C—1"

A—1¼" DIA
CLOSET POLE
C—¾" DIA
DOWEL

A—¾" O.D. × 55⅛" LG PIPE
C—⅜" O.D. × 34¼" LG
METAL ROD

A—45"
C—28"

A—39"
C—25"

A—93¼"
C—58⁵⁄₃₂"

A—32⅜"
C—20¼"

A—42"
C—26½"

A—1½"
C—1"
OVERHANG
(TYP)

82°

A—8⅜"
C—5¼"

A—71½"
C—44⅝"

A—76½"
C—47¾"

END VIEW

A—ADULT SIZE
C—CHILD SIZE

Note: Although this project is not difficult to make, it has a lot of parts. Furthermore, many of the parts are similar. To avoid confusion, we suggest you build it in three stages — frame, swings and platform, and sunshade. This will make it easier to keep track of the pieces.

Making the Frame

1 **Select the stock and cut the frame parts to size.** To make the child-size version of this glider, you need about 44 board feet of 4/4 (four-quarters) stock, and eight ¾″-diameter x 36″ dowels. Select *clear* lumber, with straight grain and no knots. Because most of the parts are very slender, knots and other defects may weaken the glider. You can use any cabinet-grade wood, although hardwoods will wear better. The glider shown is made of oak.

You can make the adult version from construction-grade one-by and two-by stock, so long as you pick through the piles and select boards with solid knots and no splits or checks. Choose pressure-treated lumber, particularly for the legs. You'll need nine 10′-long 2 x 4s, fifteen 8′-long 2 x 4s, nine 8′-long 1 x 12s, and four 1¼″-diameter x 8′ closet poles.

If you are making the child-size glider, plane 6 board feet of 4/4 stock to ⅞″ thick to make the back splats and seat slats, and 10 board feet to ⅜″ thick to make the sunshade slats. Plane the remaining stock to ¾″ thick. (If you're making the adult-size glider, you needn't do any planing.)

Cut the frame parts to the sizes shown in the Materials List. Miter the ends of the stretchers and stiffeners at 82°. Also, miter the bottom ends of the legs at 67° as shown in the *Leg Layout,* the top ends of the braces at 16°, and the bottom ends of the braces at 82°, as shown in the *Brace Layout.*

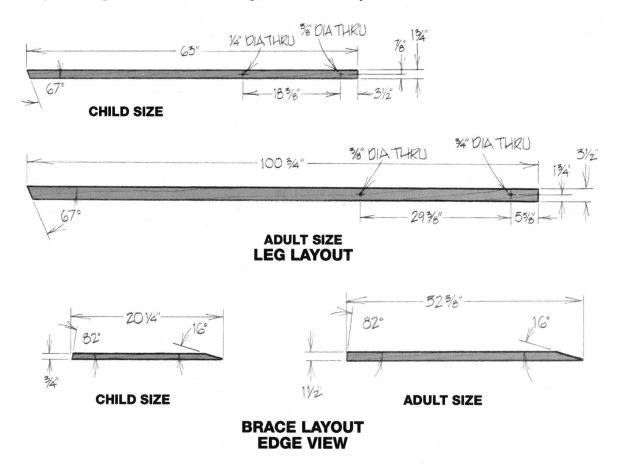

CHILD SIZE

ADULT SIZE
LEG LAYOUT

CHILD SIZE   ADULT SIZE

BRACE LAYOUT
EDGE VIEW

2

Cut the shapes of the spacers. The spacers are large, thick rings of wood, like oversize washers. Scribe the circular shape with a compass, then cut the shapes with a band saw or saber saw. Sand the sawed edges.

3

Drill the holes in the frame parts. Many of the parts in this project are duplicates — they're cut and drilled exactly the same. To make sure they all match, pad drill them — stack them face to face, tape the stack together, then drill through the entire stack.

The legs, cross ties, and spacers are three such parts. Stack them in three separate stacks and tape the stacks together. Measure and mark the locations of the holes on the top part in each stack, as shown on the *Leg Layout, Cross Tie Layout,* and *Spacer Detail.* Drill the holes, then take the stacks apart and discard the tape.

Note: Because the legs slope both front-to-back and side-to-side, many of the bolts must pass through the

TRY THIS! To keep the parts in a stack from shifting as you drill them, hold the stack together with double-faced carpet tape.

frame parts at compound angles. It's unnecessarily tedious and complex to calculate all these angles, then set up your equipment to drill them. Instead, drill all the holes perpendicular to the faces of the boards. Later, when you assemble the frame, you can ream the holes with a slightly larger drill bit so the bolts will fit.

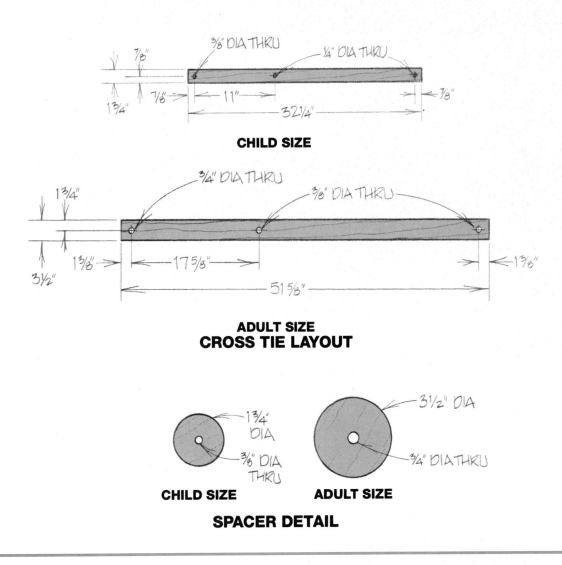

CHILD SIZE

ADULT SIZE
CROSS TIE LAYOUT

CHILD SIZE   **ADULT SIZE**

SPACER DETAIL

4 Assemble the frame.

Assemble the frame. Lightly sand the frame parts to remove any rough spots. Assemble the legs, stretchers, braces, and stiffeners with spiral nails. To prevent the parts from splitting, drill pilot holes for the nails before you drive them.

Assemble each pair of cross ties with ¼" x 2" hex bolts or ⅜" x 3½" carriage bolts, flat washers, and stop nuts. Place a washer *between* each wooden part, as shown on the *Pivot Assembly Detail,* as well as on the ends of the bolts. This will keep the parts from rubbing.

Note: If you're assembling a child-size glider with hex bolts, you'll need *three* washers for each pivot joint — one washer between the wooden parts and one on either end of the bolt. For an adult-size glider, in which you're using carriage bolts, you'll just need *two* washers per joint — one between the wooden parts and one over the threaded end of the bolt.

If you're building the child-size glider, cut the ⅜"-diameter metal rods to 34½" long. Using a die, cut ⅜-16 threads on the ends of the rods. (See Figure 1.) If you're making the adult size, have a plumbing supplier cut two ¾" O.D. pipes 55⅛" long, then thread both ends. Purchase pipe nuts to fit the threaded ends.

Note: If you don't have a die to cut the threads on the metal rods, use push nuts on the ends — these don't require threads. However, push nuts aren't as easy to remove as stop nuts. Should the glider need repair, it will be more difficult to replace parts.

Ream the holes near the tops of the legs with a bit that's about ¹⁄₆₄" larger than the metal rod (or pipe). As you ream, re-drill the holes at a slight angle, parallel to the top frame stretchers. (See Figure 2)

Insert the metal rods (or pipes) through these holes. If they're tight, ream the holes again with a slightly larger bit. Put the spacers over the ends of the rods, one on each side of the assembly.

Ream the holes in the top ends of the cross ties, then put them over the rods. Secure them with washers and nuts, but do *not* tighten the nuts yet. You'll need to remove them when you hang the swings.

Line up the bottom ends of the cross ties with the appropriate holes in the legs. Ream *both* the cross ties and the legs, then secure the parts with hex (or carriage) bolts, washers, and wing nuts. (See Figure 3.)

1/Cut threads on the ends of the metal rods with a die. The threaded sections should be about ½" long.

2/Because the legs slope front-to-back and top-to-bottom, you must re-drill some of the bolt holes at compound angles when you assemble the frame. Drill the holes that hold the metal rods (or pipes) so they're parallel to the top frame stretchers.

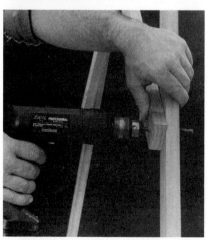

3/As best you can, line up the holes in the bottom ends of the cross ties with the appropriate holes in the legs. Re-drill both parts at once.

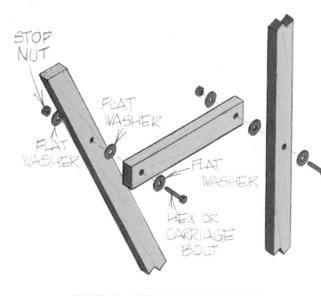

STOP NUT

FLAT WASHER

FLAT WASHER

FLAT WASHER

HEX OR CARRIAGE BOLT

PIVOT ASSEMBLY DETAIL

Making the Swings and Platform

5 **Cut the swing and platform parts to size.** Cut the swing and platform parts to the sizes shown in the Materials List. If you're making a child-size glider, rip the back and seat slats from the 7/8"-thick stock. (The thickness of the stock will become the width of the slats.) Rip the slats slightly wider than 3/8", then plane them to remove the saw marks.

6 **Drill the holes in the swing supports, back supports, arms, seat supports, and platform supports.** Make five stacks, one each for the swing supports, back supports, arms, seat supports, and platform supports. Tape the stacks together. On the top part in each stack, measure and mark the locations of the holes, as shown in the *Swing Support Layout, Back Layout, Arm Layout, Seat Layout,* and *Platform Layout.*

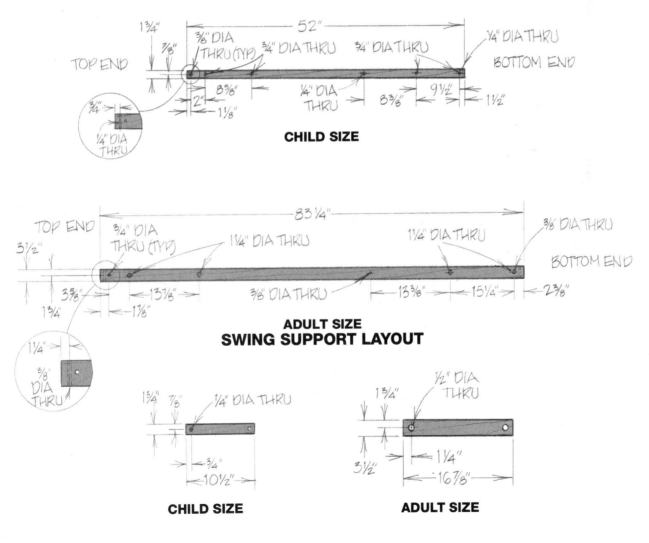

SWING SUPPORT LAYOUT

ARM LAYOUT

Also, mark the notches on the back support and platform support. It's easier to make the blind ends of these notches by drilling holes than by cutting the radii with a band saw or saber saw.

Drill the holes, then take the swing support, arm, and seat support stacks apart and discard the tape. Don't take the back support or platform support stacks apart yet.

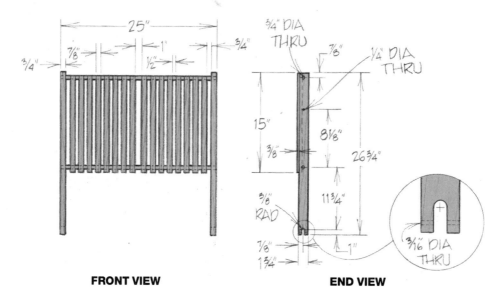

FRONT VIEW   **END VIEW**

CHILD SIZE

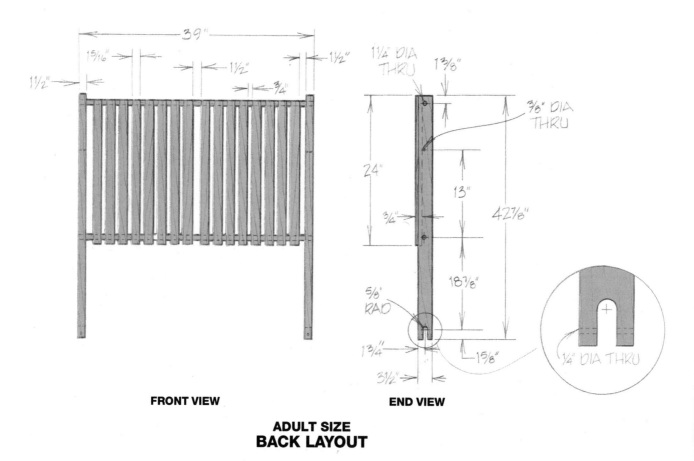

FRONT VIEW   **END VIEW**

ADULT SIZE
BACK LAYOUT

The swing supports carry a great deal of weight. For this reason, they are reinforced with carriage bolts near the bottom and top ends, as shown in the *Top Pivot Detail*. Turn the supports 90° and drill holes in their edges for these bolts. Also drill holes in the edges of the back supports, near the bottom ends, for the cotter pins (or carriage bolts) that fasten the back supports to the platform stretchers. You can drill these holes without taking the back support stack apart.

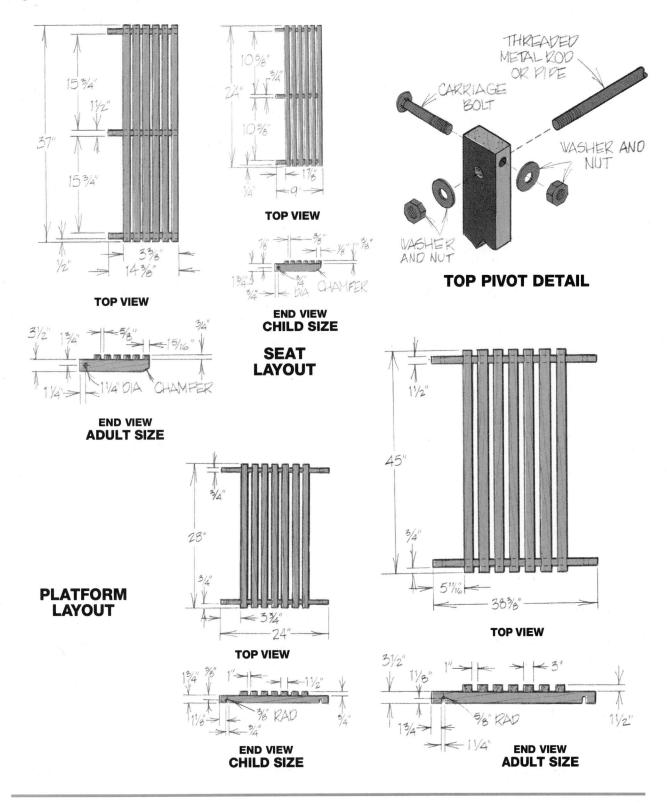

TOP PIVOT DETAIL

SEAT LAYOUT

PLATFORM LAYOUT

7 **Open the notches.** To complete the notches on the back supports and platform supports, saw the edges with a band saw or saber saw. This will open each notch on one end. (See Figure 4.) Take the stacks apart and discard the tape.

4/To make a notch, first drill a hole at the blind end. Then open up the other end with a band saw or saber saw.

8 **Assemble the swings and platform.** Lightly sand the swing and platform parts to remove any rough spots.

Attach the seat slats to the seat supports, spacing them as shown in the *Seat Layout.* Insert a back stretcher dowel (or closet pole) through the holes in the seat supports of each seat assembly. Then insert the back stretcher in the back support. Fasten the stretchers in place by driving finishing nails through them and into the dowels. The ends of the dowels must be flush with the outside faces of the supports. Attach the back slats to the back supports with finishing nails, spacing the slats as shown in the *Back Layout/Front View.*

Insert the platform stretcher dowels (or closet poles) in the holes in the swing supports. Fasten them in place with finishing nails, as you did the back stretchers. As before, the ends of the stretchers must be flush with the outside edges of the supports. Also, insert the carriage bolts in the edge holes near the ends of the supports. Secure the bolts with washers and nuts.

Attach one end of the arms to the swing supports with hex (or carriage) bolts, flat washers, and stop nuts. Then attach the other ends to the back supports in the same manner. Since these are pivoting joints, place washers between the wooden parts.

Slip the notched ends of the back supports over the bottom platform stretcher. Insert cotter pins (or 1/4" x 4" carriage bolts) through the holes in the bottom ends of the back supports to keep them in place.

Attach the platform slats to the platform supports using finishing nails. Space them as shown in the *Platform Layout.* Set the heads of all the finishing nails, not only on the platform but also on the back and seat assemblies.

9 **Hang the swings and platform.** Remove one of the metal rods (or pipes) from the frame assembly. Put a swing assembly in place with the swing seat facing in, and replace the rod. Repeat for the other swing. Then secure the metal rods with washers and nuts.

Place the platform assembly over the bottom platform stretchers, resting the stretchers in the notches. This will tie the swing assemblies together so they move in unison.

Making the Sunshade

10 **Cut the sunshade parts to size.** Cut the sunshade parts to the sizes shown in the Materials List. Bevel the top edges of the sunshade supports at 20°, as shown in the *Sunshade/End View.* Also, bevel the bottom edges of the outside sunshade slats and the top edges of the middle slats at the same angle.

11

Cut the shapes of the trusses. Lay out the shapes of the trusses as shown in the *Sun-* shade Truss Layout. Cut the shapes with a band saw or a saber saw. Sand the sawed edges.

12

Cut the notches in the sunshade supports. Stack the sunshade supports and tape them together. Mark the locations of the notches on the top part in the stack, as shown in the *Sunshade* *Support Layout*. Drill holes to make the blind ends of the notches, then saw the edges with a saber saw or coping saw to open the other ends. Take the stack apart and discard the tape.

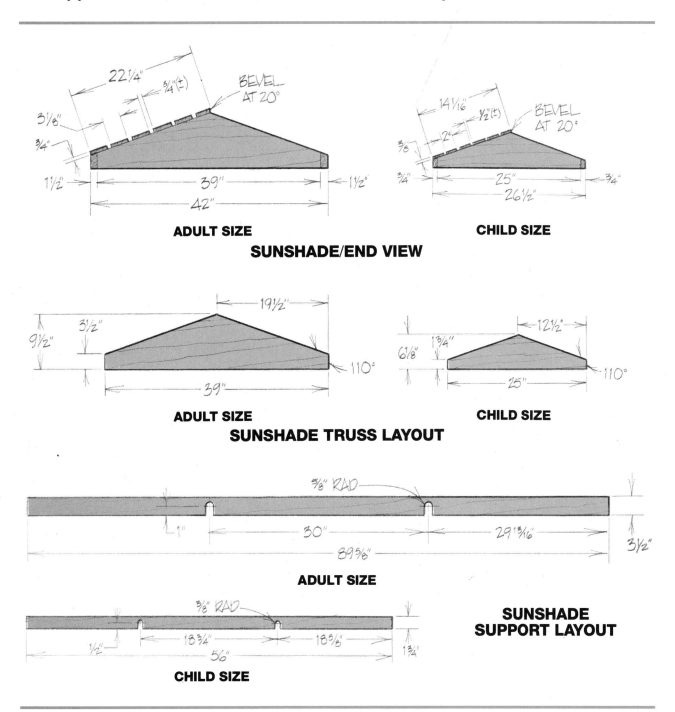

ADULT SIZE   **CHILD SIZE**

SUNSHADE/END VIEW

ADULT SIZE   **CHILD SIZE**

SUNSHADE TRUSS LAYOUT

ADULT SIZE

**SUNSHADE
SUPPORT LAYOUT**

CHILD SIZE

13 **Assemble the sunshade.** Attach the sunshade supports to the trusses with spiral nails. To prevent the parts from splitting, drill pilot holes for the nails. Attach the slats to the trusses with finishing nails, spacing them as shown in the *Sunshade/End View*. Set the heads of the nails.

14 **Hang the sunshade.** Set the sunshade assembly on the top middle platform stretchers, so the stretchers rest in the notches.

With all the parts in place, test the swinging action of the glider. The swings should move back and forth in unison. As they do so, the platform and the sunshade should remain level.

Note: For safety, the sunshade limits the travel of the glider — if you swing too far, the top of the sunshade will hit the top platform stretcher dowel. This prevents someone from swinging so high that they tip the glider over. Keep the sunshade in place whenever the glider is in use, especially if it's used by children.

Finishing Up

15 **Finish the glider.** Disassemble the glider, detaching all the subassemblies. Remove all the metal hardware and set it aside. Do any necessary touch-up sanding, then apply at least two coats of exterior paint or another finish to the wooden surfaces. After the last coat of finish dries, reassemble the glider and set it in your yard.

To store the glider, you don't have to completely disassemble it. Simply remove the sunshade and platform by lifting them off their stretchers. Loosen the bolts that hold the bottom ends of the cross ties to the legs, and remove the cotter pins (or carriage bolts) that hold the bottom ends of the back supports to the stretchers. Then fold the swings and glider frame flat.

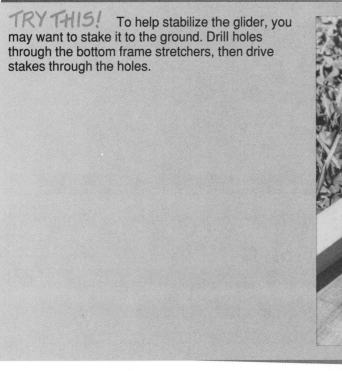

TRY THIS! To help stabilize the glider, you may want to stake it to the ground. Drill holes through the bottom frame stretchers, then drive stakes through the holes.

Shaker Bench

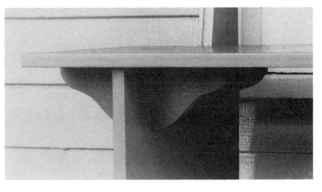

The design for this bench originated over 150 years ago, in the Shaker community of Hancock, Massachusetts. At the time, it was an innovative design — a light, easy-to-move trestle bench with a back. It was originally used indoors, in the Shakers' communal dining hall. However, it also serves well on a porch, in a garden — almost anywhere outdoors.

Like most Shaker furniture, it's very simple to build. There are few parts and little joinery. Consequently, there are few places where moisture will accumulate, and this helps to keep it from deteriorating when left out in the weather. If you protect it with an exterior finish, it will last indefinitely.

Materials List

FINISHED DIMENSIONS

PARTS

A. Seat $7/8'' \times 13'' \times 78''$
B. Backrest $7/8'' \times 4'' \times 78''$
C. Legs (3) $7/8'' \times 16\frac{1}{2}'' \times 34\frac{1}{4}''$
D. Braces (6) $7/8'' \times 4'' \times 12\frac{1}{2}''$

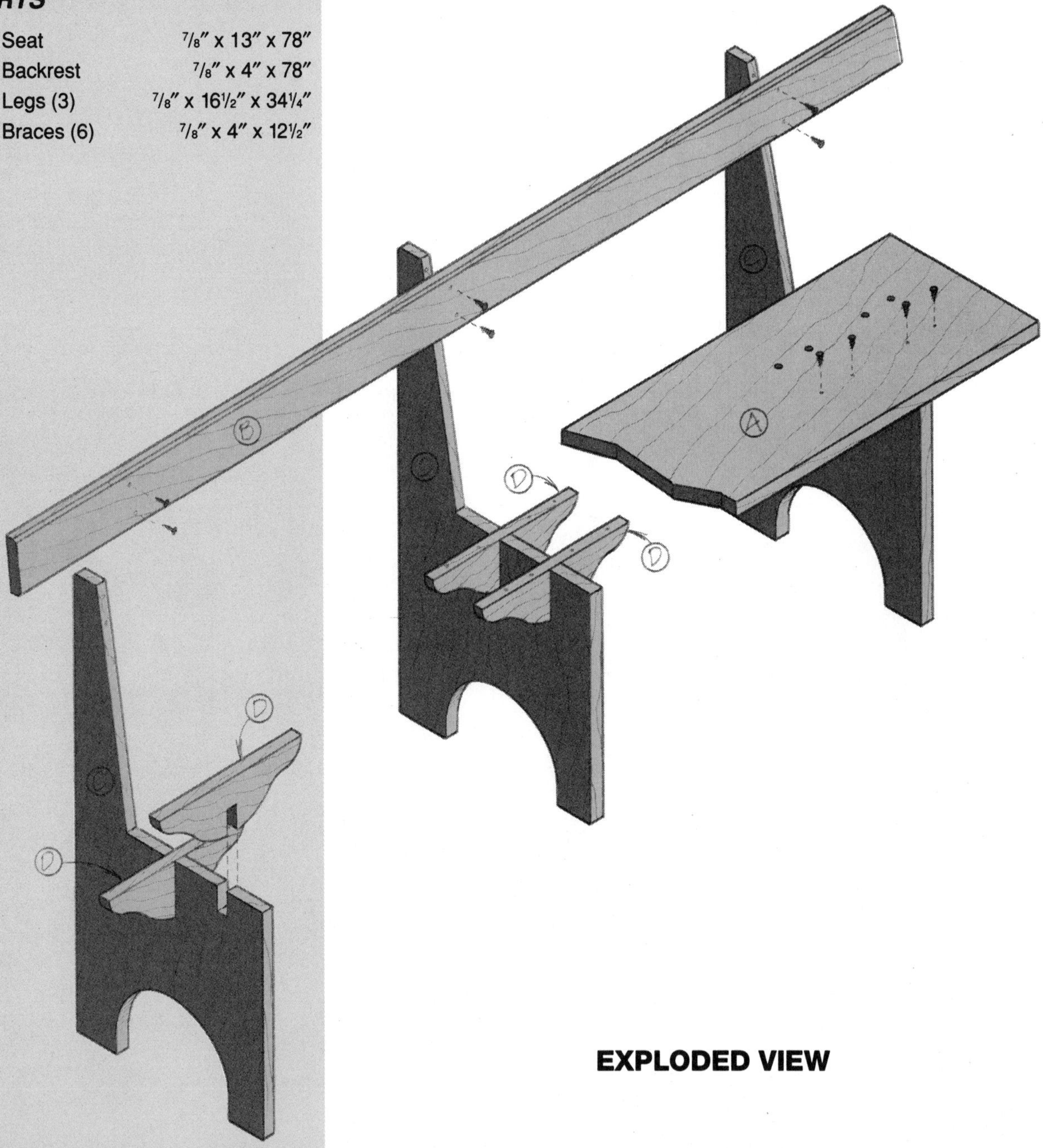

HARDWARE

#10 x 2" Brass flathead wood screws
  (27)

EXPLODED VIEW

1

Select the stock and cut the parts to size. To make this project, you need about 26 board feet of 4/4 (four-quarters) stock. You can use almost any cabinet-grade wood, but Shaker craftsmen traditionally used white pine, poplar, maple, or birch to make benches. The bench shown is made from white pine, and the original was made from poplar.

After selecting the stock, plane it all to 7/8″ thick. Glue up the stock needed to make the wide parts — the seat and legs. Cut all the parts to the sizes shown in the Materials List.

2

Cut the shapes of the legs and braces. Since you must make identical copies of the shaped parts — three legs and six braces — stack the wood so you can cut duplicates. Make two stacks, one for the legs and the other for the braces. Arrange the boards in each stack so the edges and ends are flush. Stick the parts together with double-faced carpet tape. (See Figure 1.)

Lay out the shape of the legs on the top board in the leg stack, as shown in the *Leg Layout*. Enlarge the *Brace Pattern* and trace it onto the top board in the brace stack. Note that these two parts fit together with lap joints. Each brace has one 7/8″-wide, 2″-long notch, and each leg has two.

Cut the shapes and the notches with a band saw or fretsaw. (You can also use a saber saw, but you won't be able to cut more than two parts at once.) While the parts are still stacked, sand the sawed edges smooth. However, *don't* sand the insides of the notches. After sanding, take the stacks apart and discard the tape.

1/When sawing and sanding duplicate parts, assemble the stack with double-faced carpet tape. Rub the parts with a tack cloth to remove the sawdust before you apply the tape — otherwise the tape may not adhere properly.

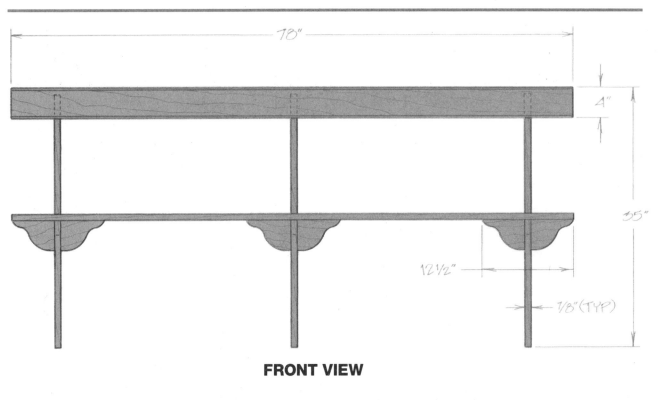

FRONT VIEW

3 **Chamfer the backrest.** As shown in the *Backrest Profile,* the front corners of the backrest are chamfered. This helps make the bench more comfortable. Cut the 45° chamfers with a table saw, jointer, router, or plane. (See Figure 2.)

*2/Shaker crafts-men cut the chamfer in the backrest with a **chamfer plane.** This handy tool is still available today. It looks and works like a spoke-shave. Grip it in both hands and draw it along the edge of the wood.*

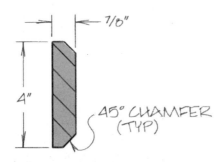

BACKREST PROFILE

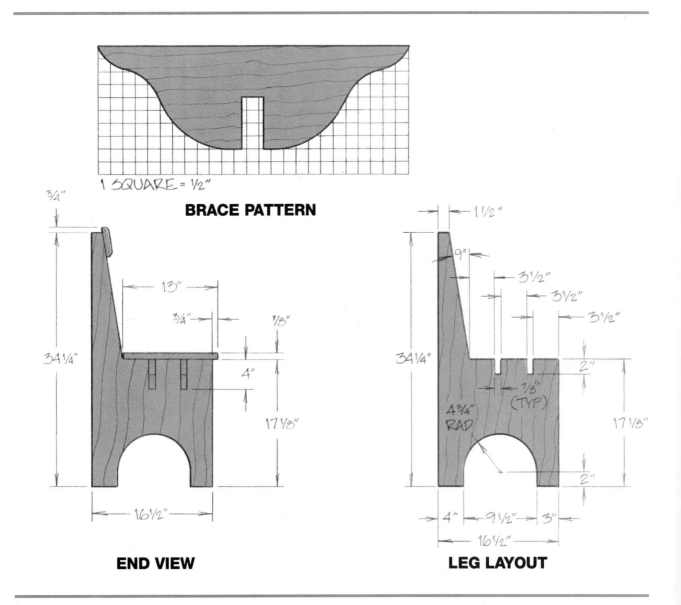

1 SQUARE = ½"

BRACE PATTERN

END VIEW

LEG LAYOUT

4 **Assemble the bench.** Finish sand all the parts. Dry assemble the legs and braces. Make sure that the top edge of each brace is *precisely* even with the top edge of the leg. If you've cut the notches too deep, shim them so the surfaces are flush. If they're too shallow, cut them a little deeper.

Glue the braces to the legs. If this bench will be used outdoors, use a waterproof glue such as resorcinol or epoxy. Let the glue dry, then attach the seat and backrest to the legs with screws. Counterbore and countersink the screws, then cover the heads with wooden plugs. Sand the plugs flush with the wood surface.

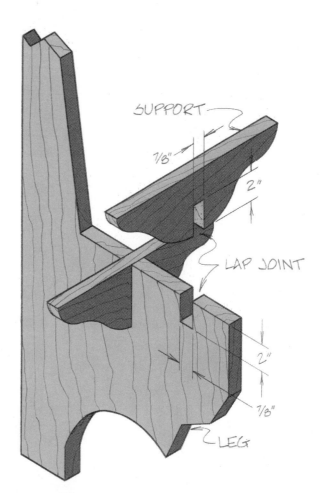

SUPPORT-TO-LEG JOINERY DETAIL

5 **Finish the bench.** Round over or "break" the hard edges and corners on the seat with sandpaper, so these won't bite into the backs of people's legs when they sit on the bench. Do any necessary touch-up sanding, then apply paint or a finish to the completed project. (Traditionally, these benches were painted either red or blue.)

If you plan to use the bench outdoors, coat the wood with a waterproof sealant before you finish it. Give the bottoms of the legs an extra coat to prevent water from soaking into the feet. Then apply an exterior paint or other finish. Be careful to coat *all* sides of the project — front and back, top and bottom — evenly.

Child's Garden Bench

A piece of children's furniture often makes a useful and interesting accent, whether you have kids or not. This bench is a good example. It's designed as a seat for toddlers, but it will also serve as an attractive plant stand or step stool for your porch, patio, or garden.

The bench shown is patterned after an old English "settle," the forerunner of contemporary sofas. Settles were often built entirely from broad, flat planks and nailed together — more a carpenter's project than a cabinetmaker's. This project is no different. Simply make a few straightforward joints, cut out the shapes of the various parts, and assemble it with nails or screws.

Materials List

FINISHED DIMENSIONS

PARTS

A.	Sides (2)	$5/8'' \times 12'' \times 25''$
B.	Back	$5/8'' \times 22\frac{1}{2}'' \times 24\frac{1}{4}''$
C.	Seat	$5/8'' \times 12'' \times 26\frac{1}{2}''$
D.	Apron	$5/8'' \times 4'' \times 25\frac{7}{8}''$
E.	Ledger	$5/8'' \times 1\frac{1}{2}'' \times 22\frac{1}{4}''$
F.	Glue blocks (2)	$5/8'' \times 5/8'' \times 3''$
G.	Fillers (2)	$5/16'' \times 5/8'' \times 4\frac{1}{4}''$

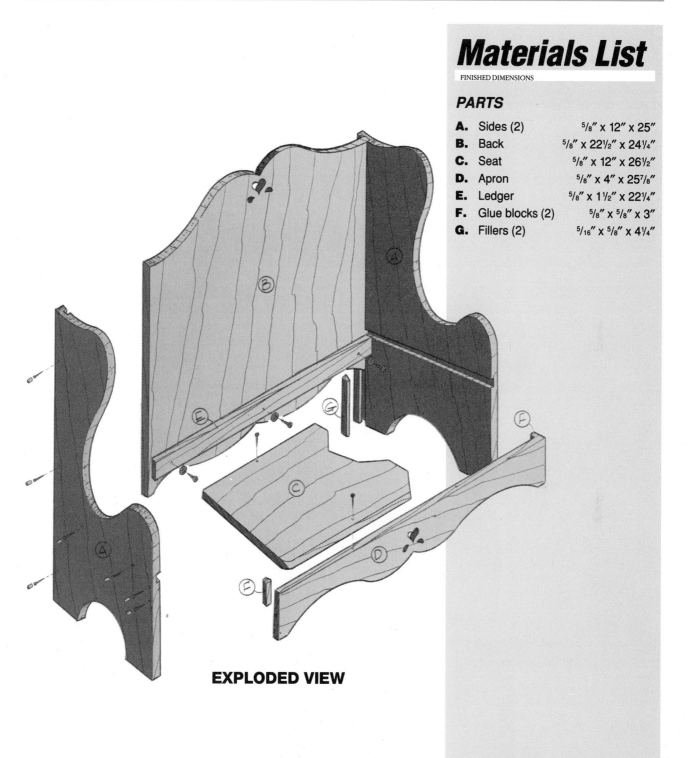

EXPLODED VIEW

HARDWARE

#8 x 1¼" Flathead wood screws
   (16–18)
#8 x 1¼" Roundhead wood screws (3)
#8 Flat washers (3)

1 ***Select the stock and cut the parts to
size.*** To make this project, you need about 14
board feet of 4/4 (four-quarters) stock. You can use
almost any cabinet-grade wood. However, if you place
this project outdoors, white pine, white or red cedar,
redwood, mahogany, and teak will weather best. The
bench shown is made from white pine.

Plane all the stock to ⅝″ thick. Cut the parts to the
sizes shown in the Materials List, except the apron and
ledger. Cut these about 1″ longer than specified. Bevel
one edge of the glue blocks at 80°, as shown in the
Glue Block Detail. Also, bevel one face of each filler
at 80°, as shown in the *Filler Detail.*

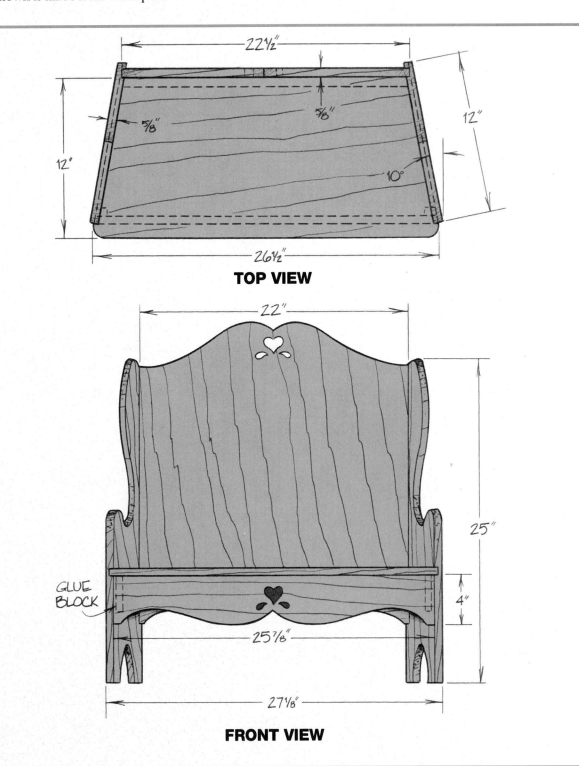

TOP VIEW

FRONT VIEW

2 Cut the joinery in the bench sides.

Cut the dadoes and grooves in the sides *before* you cut the sides to shape. Otherwise, it will be difficult to make these joints accurately. Make the grooves for the back first. These must be cut on a table saw with a dado accessory — this will allow you to tilt the table or cutter. (You cannot tilt a router bit.) Adjust the angle to 10°, and raise the cutter so the *high* side is 5⁄16″ above the table. Cut a 5⁄8″-wide, 5⁄16″-deep angled groove in each side, near the back edge. (See Figure 1.) Remember, these grooves must be mirror images of each other, as shown in the *Top View*.

Cut the 5⁄8″-wide, 5⁄16″-deep dadoes for the seat with either a dado cutter or router. (These joints are *not* angled.) Since the dadoes are blind, you may find it easier to use a router — it's simpler to tell when to stop cutting. Start the dado at the front edge of each board, then halt it just as you reach the angled groove for the back. Use a chisel to clean up the blind end of the dado where it joins the groove.

1/Cut the grooves for the back with a dado cutter. Tilt the table or cutter to 10°, so the bottom of each groove will be at an angle to the face of the board.

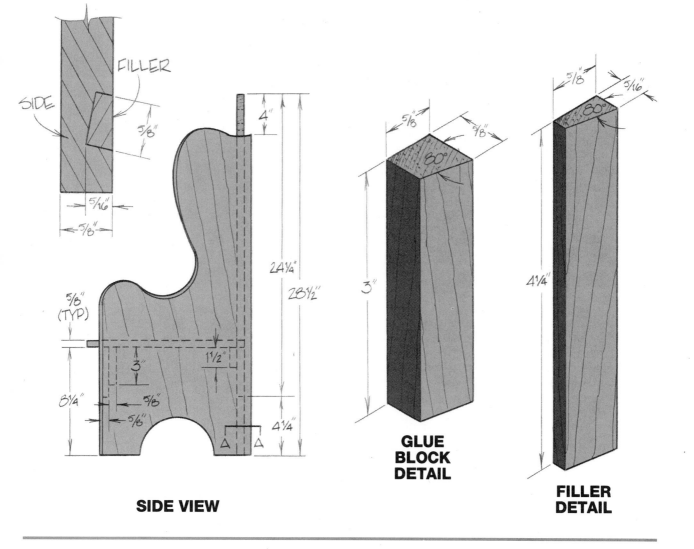

SIDE VIEW

GLUE BLOCK DETAIL

FILLER DETAIL

3 **Taper the seat.** The bench seat is trapezoid-shaped — it tapers 10° front to back, and the front corners are slightly rounded. Lay out the seat as shown in the *Seat Layout,* then cut the shape with a band saw or saber saw. Cut a little wide of the lines, then sand up to them with a disk sander or belt sander.

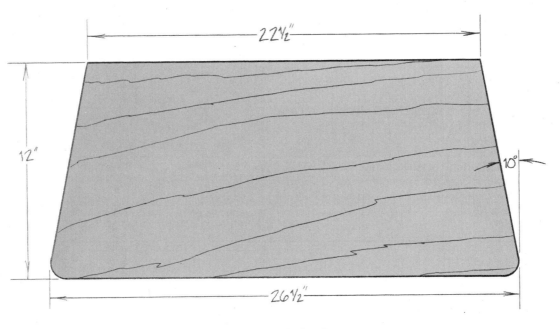

SEAT LAYOUT

4 **Fit the apron and ledger.** Temporarily dry assemble the sides, seat, and back with flathead wood screws. Counterbore and countersink the screws so you can cover the heads later. Do not glue the parts together yet. You must disassemble the bench after you fit the apron and ledger.

Cut the apron and brace to length, fitting them to the assembly. Miter the ends at 10°, cutting them just a little long. Then trim one end of each part $1/32''$–$1/16''$ at a time. After each cut, check the fit. When the piece fits properly, stop cutting. Counterbore and countersink the screws.

5 **Cut the shapes of the sides, back, and apron.** Disassemble the bench. Enlarge the *Side Pattern, Back Pattern,* and *Apron Pattern.* Trace these patterns onto the stock, then cut the shapes with a saber saw or coping saw. To make each cutout, first drill a $1/2''$-diameter hole through the waste. Insert the blade of the saw through the hole and cut to the pattern lines. Then saw out the waste. Sand or file the sawed edges smooth.

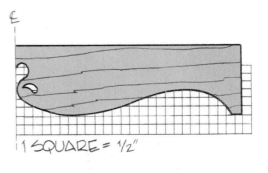

1 SQUARE = $1/2''$

APRON PATTERN

6

Assemble the bench. Glue the fillers in the grooves in the sides, as shown in *Section A*. The bottom end of each filler must be flush with the bottom end of the sides. Let the glue dry, then sand the fillers flush with the surface of the sides.

Finish sand the sides, back, seat, and apron. Glue the back to the sides, reinforcing it with flathead wood screws. Attach the ledger to the back with roundhead wood screws and flat washers, but do *not* glue it in place. The wood grains of the two parts oppose each other. If you glue the ledger in place, the back will not be able to expand and contract properly. Instead, drill oversize pilot holes in the ledger to allow the back to

move. Tighten the screws so they're snug, but not so tight that the washers begin to bite into the wood.

Glue the seat to the sides and the ledger, but *not* to the back. Also, glue the apron to the sides and seat. Reinforce the joints between the apron and the sides with glue blocks. Then reinforce all the glue joints with flathead wood screws. Counterbore and countersink the screw heads.

Cover all the exposed flathead screw heads with wood plugs, gluing the plugs in the counterbores. Let the glue dry, then sand the plugs flush with the wood surface. The bench will look as if it has been pegged together.

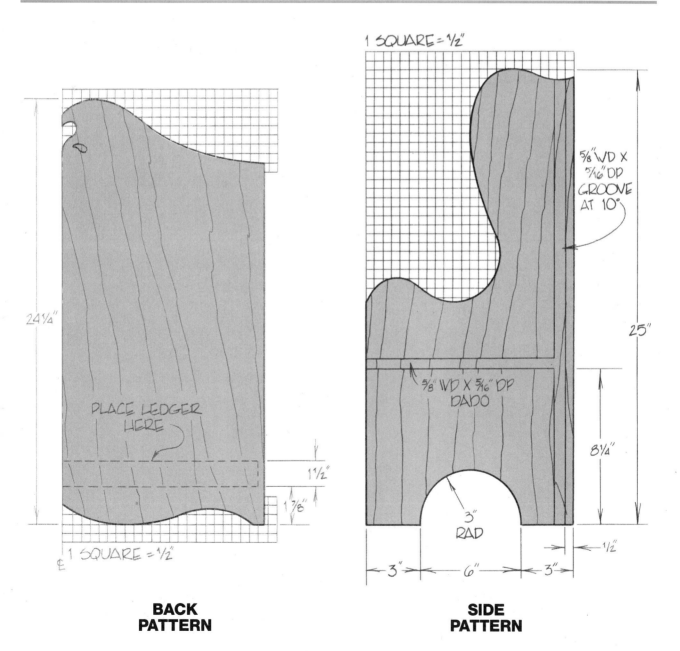

BACK PATTERN

SIDE PATTERN

7 Finish the bench. Do any necessary touch-up sanding. With a file and sandpaper, blend the top edges of the back and sides into each other. (See Figure 2.) Slightly round all the edges to give the bench a slightly worn appearance.

Coat the bottoms of the sides with a sealant to prevent them from absorbing water. Apply a finish or paint to the completed bench. Be sure to coat *all* surfaces equally to keep the boards from warping.

TRY THIS! If you want to use the bench for seating, cut a piece of 1″-thick foam rubber to fit the seat. Cover the foam with fabric to make a cushion. Sew several cords to the cushion, then drill holes in the bench so you can tie the cushion in place.

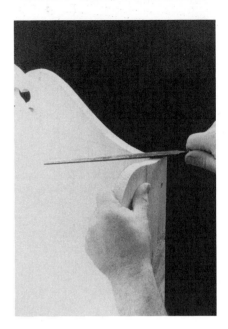

2/Blend the top edges of the sides and back together so the contours of the bench appear to be continuous. Round the edges, too. This will soften the appearance of the bench, making it appear old and worn.

Step-by-Step: Making Heart Cutouts

Country craftsmen have decorated their homes and furniture with hearts since medieval times, perhaps before. It's an ancient symbol that signifies love and family. It's also an extremely easy shape to make. You can lay out a heart with a compass, and cut it with a drill and a saber saw.

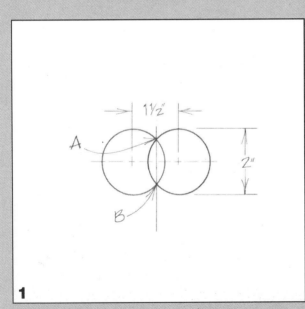

1

To lay out a heart, first draw two overlapping circles. The circles must be the same diameter, and the distance between their centers should be ¾ times their diameter. For example, if their diameters are 2″, their centers should be 1½″ apart (¾ x 2 = 1½″). Draw a vertical line through the two points (A and B) where the circles intersect.

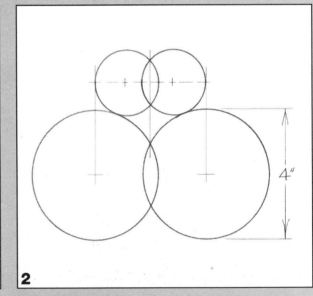

2

Draw two more lines, tangent to the circumferences of the circles and parallel to line AB. Then scribe two more overlapping circles. This second set of circles should be twice the diameter of the first. Locate the centers of these larger circles along the tangent lines so they just touch the small circles. Although these large circles will overlap themselves, they should not overlap the small circles.

(Continued)

Step-by-Step: Making Heart Cutouts — Continued

3

Erase all three lines and portions of all four circles, as indicated by the dotted lines in the drawing. The parts of the circles that are left will form a perfect heart shape.

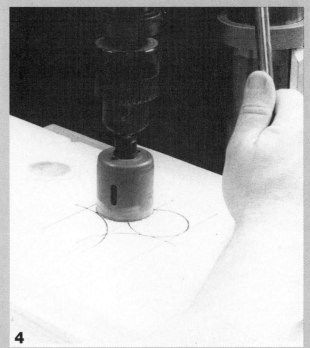

4

Cut the top portion of the heart with a drill or hole saw. Make two overlapping holes the same size and in the same position as the first two circles you drew.

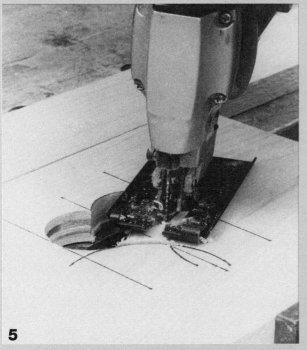

5

Cut the bottom portion with a saber saw, scroll saw, or coping saw. Insert the blade through the opening you've made and saw along the lines to remove the remainder of the waste. Smooth the sawed edges with a file.

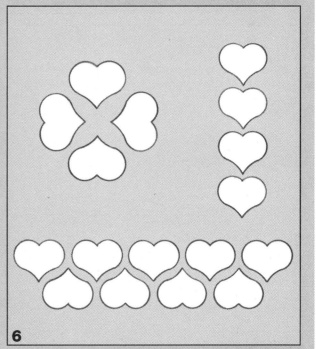

6

Because hearts were so easy to make, craftsmen sometimes cut multiple hearts to create a pattern. For example, you can arrange four hearts as shown to make a shamrock. Or, align them in different ways to create borders.

Rocking Bench

Since medieval times, it has been the custom for mothers to rock their babies. At first, they rocked them in cradles suspended between two tall posts. This proved unsafe (an energetic baby could overturn a swinging cradle) and by the sixteenth century craftsmen were mounting cradles on rockers. In the early eighteenth century, American chairmakers invented the rocking chair, and mothers began to rock the babies while holding them on their laps. Then in the nineteenth century, a southern craftsman put the two furniture forms — cradle and rocker — together.

This bench, sometimes called a "mammy bench," is a long seat on rockers, with places for an adult to sit and a baby to lay down. A mother can sit on the bench, place her baby beside her, and rock them both. This particular rocking bench is made for a child — he or she can sit and rock a doll. It also makes an excellent plant stand, knitting basket, magazine rack, or conversation piece.

This child-size bench is the handiwork of Bob Beason of Dayton, Ohio. Bob has been designing and building children's furniture since 1948 for his part-time business, Little Folks Originals. ●

Materials List

FINISHED DIMENSIONS

PARTS

A. Seat $3/4''$ x $11 1/4''$ x $31''$
B. Back $3/4''$ x $11 1/4''$ x $20 3/4''$
C. Left side $3/4''$ x $13 1/2''$ x $23 3/8''$
D. Middle $3/4''$ x $11 3/4''$ x $18 3/4''$
E. Right side $3/4''$ x $12''$ x $13''$
F. Rockers (2) $3/4''$ x $3 1/4''$ x $20 1/2''$
G. Rails (2) $3/4''$ x $1''$ x $19''$
H. Spindles (24) $1/2''$ dia. x $6''$
J. Long dowels (4) $3/8''$ dia. x $4''$
K. Short dowels (24) $1/4''$ dia. x $2''$

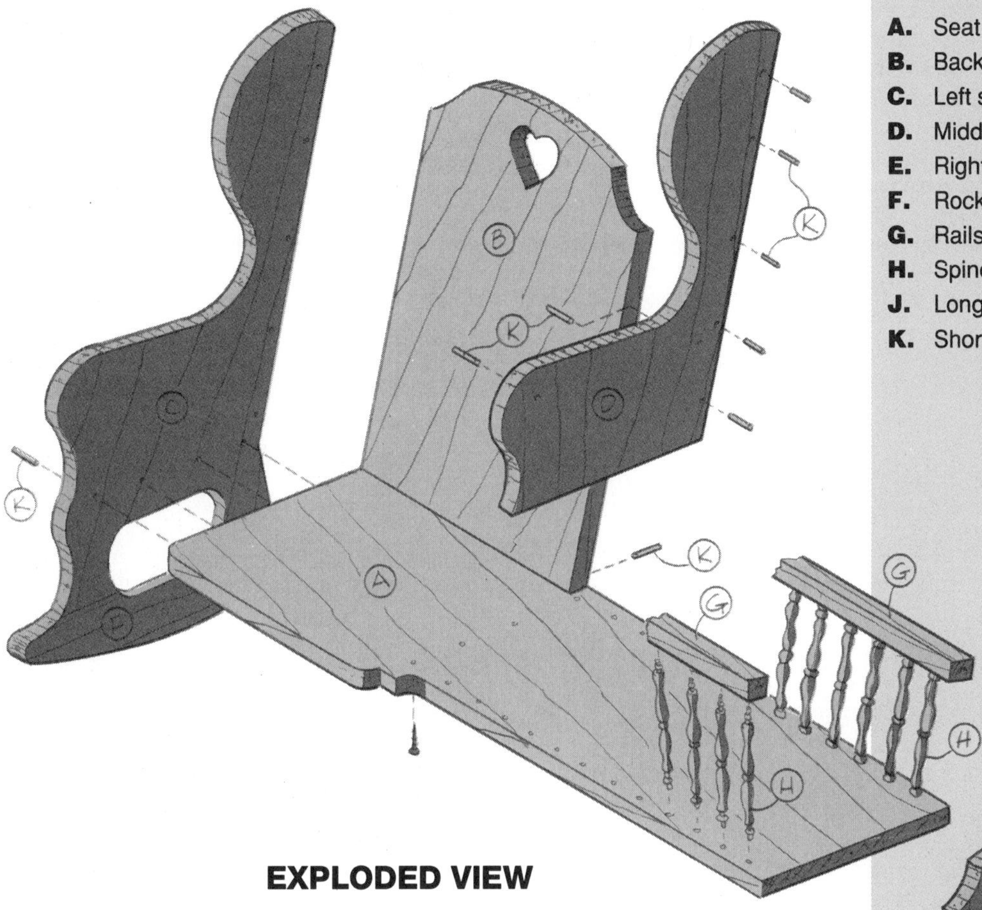

EXPLODED VIEW

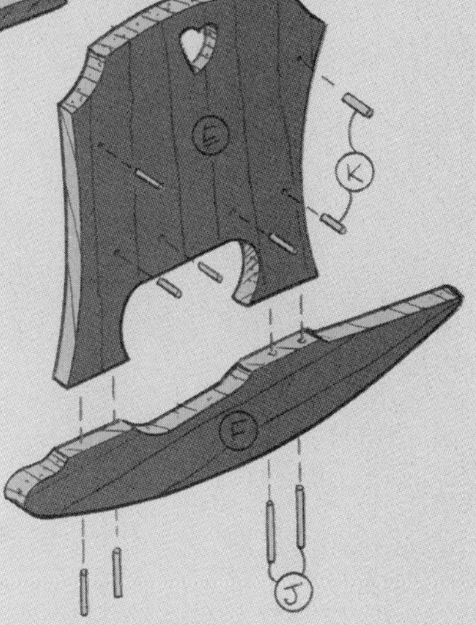

HARDWARE

2d Common nails (24–30)
#10 x $1 1/2''$ Flathead wood screws (2)

1

Select the stock and cut the parts to size.

To make this project, you need about 12 board feet of 4/4 (four-quarters) stock. You can use any cabinet-grade hardwood or softwood. (The bench shown is made of pine.) However, if you set the bench outdoors, use a weather-resistant wood such as cypress, cedar, or redwood. Avoid pressure-treated lumber, especially if this project will be used by young children who might chew on the edges.

The spindles can be purchased from several different woodworking suppliers. Here are two sources:

Meisel Hardware Specialties
P.O. Box 70
Mound, MN 55364

The Woodworker's Store
21801 Industrial Blvd.
Rogers, MN 55374

You can also turn your own. If you plan to do this, purchase *hardwood* stock, such as maple or birch. Softwood spindles will break easily.

When you've gathered the materials, plane the 4/4 stock to ¾" thick. Glue up stock to make the wide boards needed for the sides and middle. Then cut the parts to the sizes shown in the Materials List.

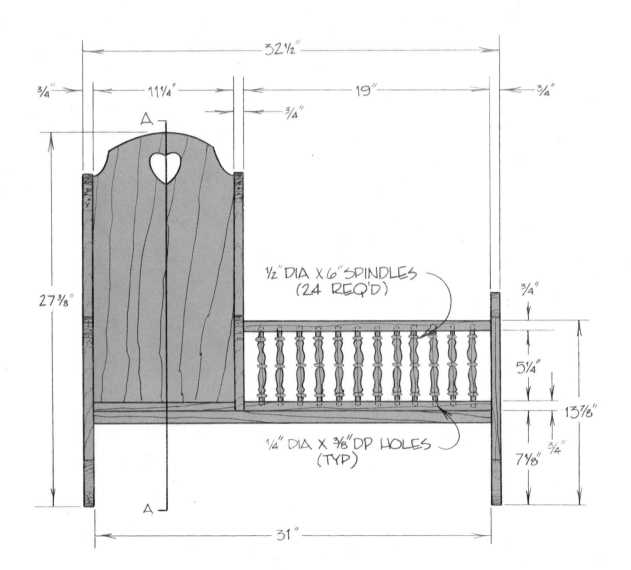

FRONT VIEW

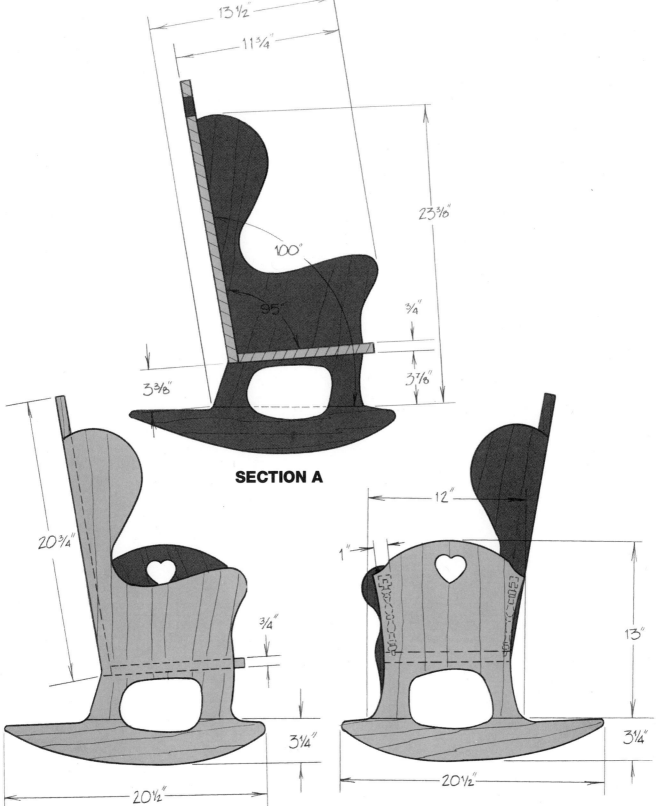

SECTION A

LEFT SIDE VIEW

RIGHT SIDE VIEW

2 **Drill the holes needed.** Lay out the shape of the seat, including the locations of the 1/4"-diameter holes, as shown in the *Seat Layout*. Also, mark the locations of the spindle holes on the bottom faces of the rails.

Drill the 3/8"-deep spindle holes in the seat and rails. Although the spindles are angled slightly toward the front and back, you can drill these holes perpendicular

to the seat surface. When you assemble the bench, the wood will give slightly, allowing you to angle the spindles.

Also, drill the two through holes in the chair portion of the seat near the back edge. If you use the bench outdoors, these holes will help to drain water off the seat. If you set it indoors, use the holes to tie a cushion to the seat.

3 **Cut the shapes of the parts.** Enlarge the *Patterns* and trace the shapes onto the right side, middle, left side, rockers, and back. Miter the bottom ends of the sides at 100° on a table saw. Then cut the outside shapes with a band saw or saber saw. To cut the inside shapes, drill a hole in the waste. Insert the blade of a saber saw or coping saw through this hole,

saw out to the pattern line, then cut out the waste.

Also cut the shape of the seat. As shown in the *Seat Layout,* the edge of the notch (where the back joins the seat) is beveled at 5°. To cut this bevel, tilt the table of the band saw or the shoe of the saber saw. Saw up to the end of the notch, then remove the waste with a dovetail saw or back saw. (See Figures 1 and 2.)

1/To cut the beveled edge of the notch in the seat, tilt the table of the band saw and cut up to the end of the notch.

2/Cut the end of the notch with a dovetail saw or back saw.

4 **Turn the spindles.** If you have elected to make your own spindles, turn them at this time. You can follow the pattern in the *Spindle Layout,* or

create your own. You can also substitute straight dowels for spindles, although this makes for a plainer-looking bench.

5 **Attach the rockers to the sides.** Glue the rockers to the bottom ends of the sides. If you plan to put the bench outside, use a waterproof glue such as epoxy or resorcinol.

Because you've glued the edge grain of the rockers to the end grain of the sides, the glue joints won't be par-

ticularly strong. You must reinforce them with dowels. Drill 3/8"-diameter holes, 4"-deep, through the bottom edge of the rockers and into the sides, as shown in the *Patterns.* Coat the long dowels with glue and drive them into the holes. When the glue dries, sand the dowels flush with the bottom edge of the rockers.

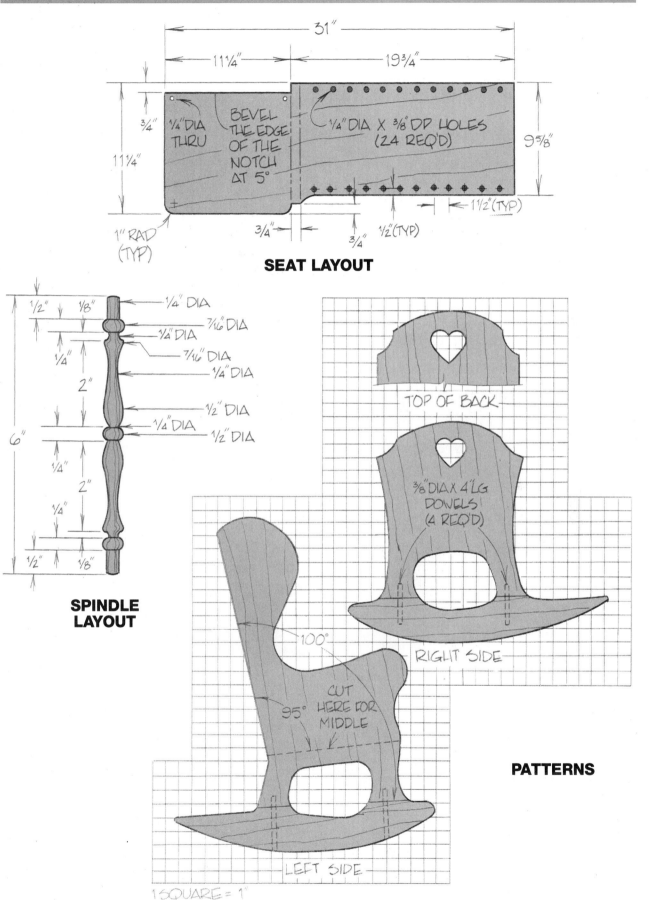

SEAT LAYOUT

SPINDLE LAYOUT

PATTERNS

1 SQUARE = 1"

6

Assemble the bench. Finish sand all the parts. Glue the spindles in the rails, then temporarily set the back spindle assembly in the seat holes. Do *not* glue it in place yet.

Attach the middle to the seat with glue, then reinforce it by driving two screws up through the seat and into the middle. Countersink the heads of the screws so they are flush with the surface of the wood. Drill a ¼″-diameter, 2″-deep hole through the middle and into the back rail. Remove the back spindle assembly from the seat.

Attach the back to the seat and the middle with glue and five evenly spaced nails. The nails will be replaced by dowels, so don't drive them all the way home; let them protrude about ½″. Allow the glue to dry. One by one, remove the nails, and drill ¼″-diameter, 2″-deep holes where they were. Coat each dowel with glue before you drive it in a hole. Then file the heads flush with the wood surface. (See Figure 3.)

Glue a dowel in the back rail where you drilled a hole earlier. Then glue the spindle assemblies (both front and back) to the seat. Drill a dowel hole through the

3/Remove the nails, one at a time, and replace them with dowels. Drill the holes for the dowels at slight angles, and vary the angle up and down or forward and back with each dowel. This will hook the parts together.

middle and into the end of the front rail. Coat a dowel with glue and drive it into the hole.

Attach the left and right sides to the bench assembly in the same manner that you attached the back — attach the parts with glue and nails, then replace the nails with dowels. File the dowels flush with the surface of the wood.

TRY THIS! There are two alternative fasteners you might use to fasten the parts of the rocking bench together. First, you could use #8 x 1¼″ flathead wood screws. Counterbore and countersink these screws, then cut short lengths of dowel to cover the heads. Glue the dowels in the counterbores and sand them flush with the surface of the wood — this will make the project look as if it were doweled together.

Second, you could use square-shanked "cut" nails. In the eighteenth and nineteenth centuries, craftsmen sometimes nailed their furniture together with hand-forged nails. These nails had square shanks, like today's cut nails. To prevent the nails from splitting the wood, drill pilot holes before you drive them. Set the heads slightly below the surface of the wood.

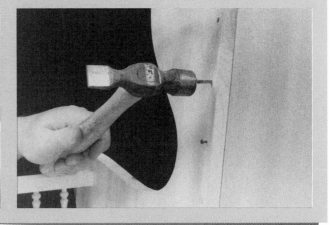

7

Finish the bench. Do any necessary touch-up sanding on the bench. Round over the edges to remove any sharp corners and give the project a soft,

worn look. Then apply a finish to the completed bench. Traditionally, benches such as these were painted.

Swing Frames

Not everyone who'd like a porch swing has a porch to put it on. No matter — your lack of a porch shouldn't prevent you from building and enjoying a swing. You can easily build a sturdy frame that will convert an ordinary porch swing into a "porchless" swing.

These are two examples of movable porchless swing frames. The tall, A-shaped frame suspends the swing from two long chains and can be placed out in the open, almost anywhere in your yard. The smaller frame converts the swing to a glider — the swing hangs from four short chains. The glider frame is low enough to be moved under a tree or roof.

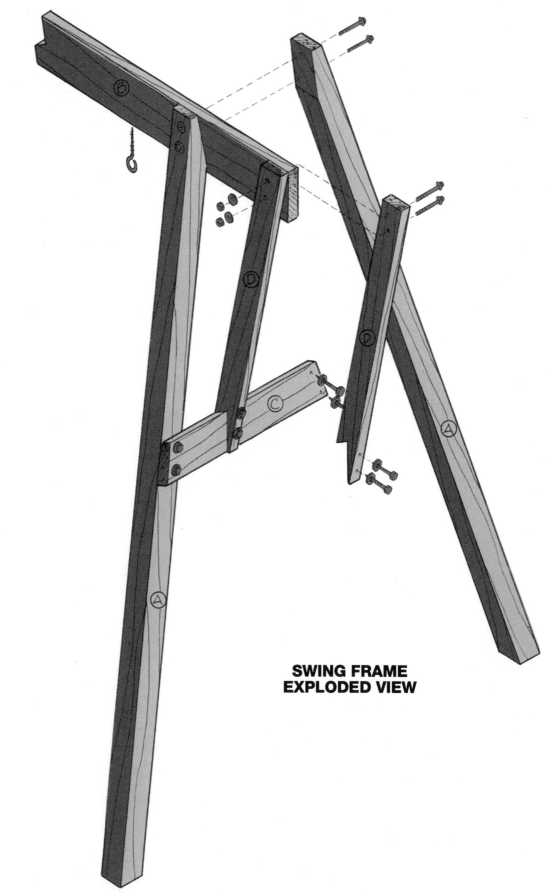

**SWING FRAME
EXPLODED VIEW**

**GLIDER FRAME
EXPLODED VIEW**

Materials List

FINISHED DIMENSIONS

PARTS

Swing Frame

A. Posts (4) $3\frac{1}{2}$" x $3\frac{1}{2}$" x $95\frac{5}{8}$"
B. Support rail $1\frac{1}{2}$" x $7\frac{1}{4}$" x 120"
C. Horizontal $1\frac{1}{2}$" x $5\frac{1}{2}$" x $27\frac{1}{2}$"
    braces (2)
D. Vertical $1\frac{1}{2}$" x $3\frac{1}{2}$" x $43\frac{1}{2}$"
    braces (4)

Glider Frame

A. Bases (2) $1\frac{1}{2}$" x $3\frac{1}{2}$" x 30"
B. Feet/ledgers (4) $1\frac{1}{2}$" x $3\frac{1}{2}$" x 24"
C. Legs (4) $1\frac{1}{2}$" x $3\frac{1}{2}$" x 33"
D. Rails (2) $1\frac{1}{2}$" x $3\frac{1}{2}$" x 76"
E. Tops (2) $1\frac{1}{2}$" x $5\frac{1}{2}$" x 30"

HARDWARE

Swing Frame

16d Common nails ($\frac{1}{2}$ lb.)
$\frac{5}{16}$" x 3" Lag screws (16)
$\frac{3}{8}$" x 5" Carriage bolts and hex nuts (4)
$\frac{3}{8}$" x 6" Carriage bolts and hex nuts (2)
$\frac{3}{8}$" x 7" Carriage bolts and hex nuts (2)
$\frac{5}{16}$" Flat washers (16)
$\frac{3}{8}$" Flat washers (8)
1" Eye screws (2)

Glider Frame

#12 x $2\frac{1}{2}$" Flathead wood screws (24–30)
#12 x $3\frac{1}{2}$" Flathead wood screws (8–12)
$\frac{5}{16}$" x 3" Lag screws (12)
$\frac{5}{16}$" Flat washers (12)
1" Eye screws (4)

Making the Swing Frame

1 Select the stock and cut the parts to size.

To make the swing frame, you need four 8'-long 4 x 4s, one 10'-long 2 x 8, one 8'-long 2 x 6, and two 8'-long 2 x 4s. Since this frame will be used outdoors, purchase pressure-treated lumber. Make sure the 4 x 4s are rated LP-22 (for ground contact). The rest of the lumber can be rated either LP-2 or LP-22.

Cut the horizontal and vertical braces about an inch longer than given in the Materials List — this will allow you room to lay out the miters. You won't need to cut the 2 x 8 rail, because it's already the size you need. Don't bother to cut the 4 x 4 posts, either. You can trim them to size when you cut the miters.

2 Cut the miters and notches.

Lay out the miters on the posts as shown in the *Post Layout,* on the horizontal braces as shown in the *End View,* and on the vertical braces as shown in the *Vertical Brace Layout.* Also, lay out the angled notches on the bottom ends of the vertical braces.

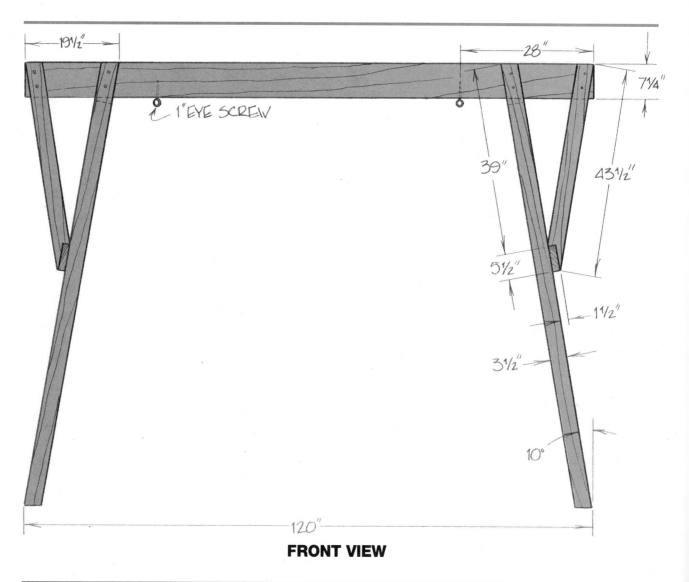

FRONT VIEW

Cut the miters with a circular saw or hand saw. (See Figures 1 and 2.) Cut the notches with a saber saw or hand saw.

*1/*Most circular saws won't cut deep enough to saw a 4 x 4 post in two with one pass. Instead, carefully mark the cut on two opposite sides of the post.

*2/*Cut one side, following the layout line. Then turn the post over and cut again.

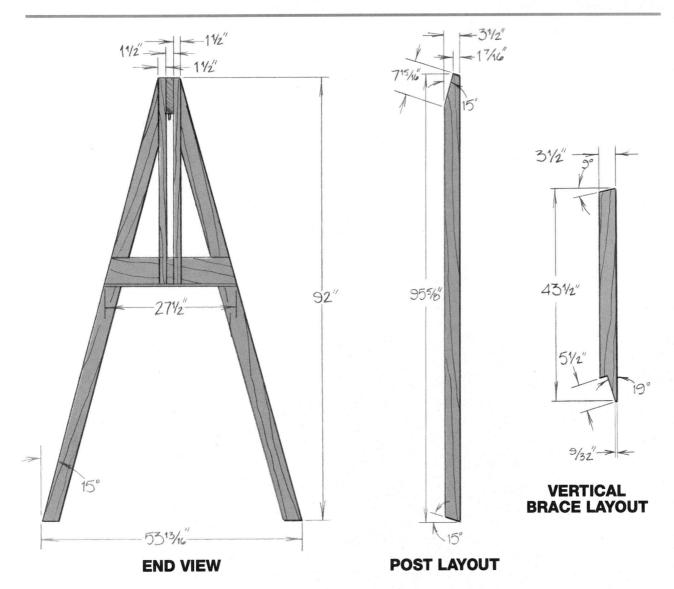

END VIEW

POST LAYOUT

VERTICAL BRACE LAYOUT

3 **Assemble the frame.** Since this is a large project, you'll need a helper or two to put it together. Also, plan to assemble it outside.

Lay the legs on a flat surface, such as your driveway. Attach the horizontal braces with 16d nails to make two A-shaped frames. The top ends of the posts should not touch; they should be 1½″ apart.

Note: *Don't* drive the nails all the way home as you assemble these parts. Hammer them in part way so you can remove them later. Also, try to drive the nails where you want to install the lag screws or carriage bolts later.)

Install the eye screws in the bottom edge of the support rail. As shown in the *Front View,* these screws are positioned for the Victorian Porch Swing. If you want to hang a different swing from this frame, you may have to change their position.

Turn the rail upside down, with the bottom edge facing up. Have a helper hold one of the post assemblies upside down. Attach it to the rail with 16d nails. Drive just *one* nail through each post, so the assemblies will pivot on the rail. Nail the vertical braces in place, then drive a few more nails through the posts and into the rail. Repeat this procedure for the other post assembly. (See Figure 3.) Once again, don't drive the nails all the way home.

Turn the assembly right side up and check that the posts hold the rail horizontal. Also check that the structure is symmetrical — each end and each side should be a mirror image of the other.

When you're satisfied the assembly is correct, replace the nails one at a time with sturdier fasteners. Drill pilot holes for the lag screws and carriage bolts as you go.

3/It's much easier to assemble the frame upside down. You can rest the rail on solid ground while you attach the posts.

Fasten the horizontal braces and the bottom ends of the vertical braces with ⁵⁄₁₆″ x 3″ lag screws, the top ends of the vertical braces with ³⁄₈″ x 5″ carriage bolts, and the posts with ³⁄₈″ x 6″ and ³⁄₈″ x 7″ carriage bolts. Secure all the bolts with nuts.

4 **Trim the top ends of the posts.** Because the posts are canted at a compound angle (15° front to back and 10° side to side), one corner or another will protrude above the top ends. Using a hand saw, trim these corners flush with the top edge of the rail. (See Figure 4.)

4/When the frame is assembled, trim the top ends of the posts even with the rail.

Making the Glider Frame

1 ***Select the stock and cut the parts to size.*** To make the glider frame, you need four 8'-long 2 x 4s and one 8'-long 2 x 6. Since this frame will be used outdoors, purchase an outdoor wood, such as cedar, redwood, or cypress. Or buy pressure-treated lumber. Make sure at least one of the 2 x 4s is rated LP-22 (for ground contact). The rest of the lumber can be rated either LP-2 or LP-22.

Note: At some lumberyards, 2 x 4 stock rated for ground contact may have to be specially ordered.

As designed, the frame will support the Victorian Porch Swing. If you want to mount another swing, you may have to adjust the length of the bases, feet, ledgers, tops, and rails. Determine the dimensions of these parts, then cut them to size. Be sure to cut the two bases from LP-22 stock.

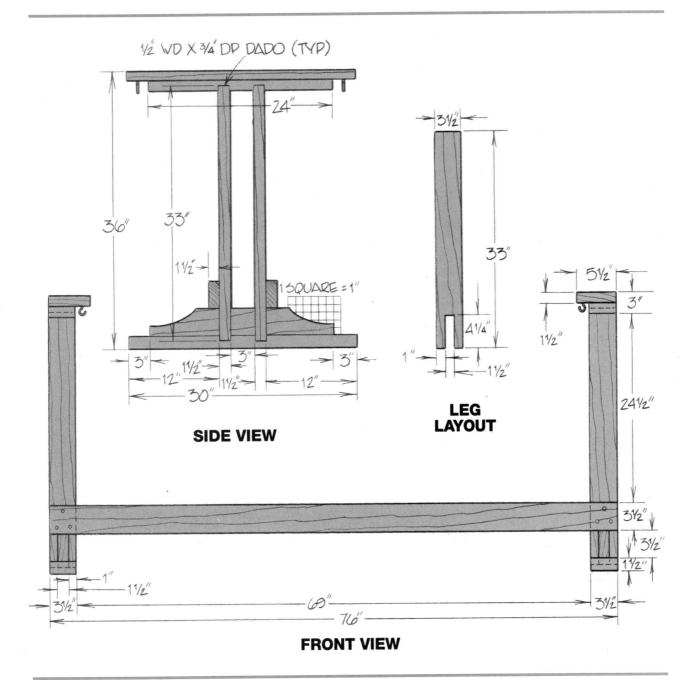

SIDE VIEW

LEG LAYOUT

FRONT VIEW

2

Cut the dadoes in the bases and ledgers. The ends of the legs are held in 1½"-wide, ¾"-deep dadoes in the bases and ledgers, as shown in the *Side View.* To make these dadoes, lay the bases and ledgers edge to edge on a flat surface. Make sure the ends of the bases are flush, and the ends of the ledgers are 3" in from the base ends. Clamp the boards together. Lay out the dadoes across all four boards.

Set a circular saw to cut exactly ¾" deep. With the boards clamped together, cut the sides of the dadoes. Also, make several kerfs through the waste. (See Figure 5.) Remove the remaining waste with a chisel. (See Figure 6.)

5/It's much quicker to make the dadoes in the bases and ledgers all at the same time. Clamp the boards edge to edge and cut the sides of the dadoes with a circular saw. Cut several kerfs in the waste to make it easier to remove.

6/Leave the boards clamped together and clean out the waste with a wide chisel.

3

Cut the notches in the legs. The bottom ends of the legs are notched to fit over the feet. Lay out these notches as shown in the *Leg Layout,* and cut them with a band saw or saber saw. You can also use a hand saw to cut the sides, then remove the waste with a coping saw.

4

Cut the shapes of the feet. Enlarge the pattern for the feet, as shown in the *Side View,* and trace it onto the stock. Cut the shapes with a band saw, saber saw, or fretsaw. Sand the sawed edges.

5

Assemble the frame. Lightly sand the parts to smooth the rough spots. (**Warning:** Always wear a dust mask when sanding pressure-treated lumber — the sawdust is toxic.) Attach the bases to the feet with #12 x 3½" flathead wood screws, then add the legs and ledgers. Drive #12 x 2½" flathead wood screws through the bases and ledgers and into the ends of the legs.

Tie the leg assemblies together with the rails, mounting the rails to the legs with lag screws and flat washers. Attach the tops to the ledgers with #12 x 2½" screws, and install the eye screws in the underside of the tops, near the inside corners.

Willow Swing

The Victorian era, like every other age, had its share of itinerant, out-of-work people. These "gypsies," as they were mistakenly called — they were no relation to migratory eastern Europeans by the same name — sometimes asked farmers for permission to camp on their land. If he was amenable, they would do whatever they could to return the favor — chop firewood, mend utensils, clean barns. Some cut willow saplings in the grove and made primitive "stick furniture" for the farmers to use outdoors or on their porches.

Although it was made from wood in its roughest form, this stick furniture was surprisingly attractive, comfortable, and sturdy. The gypsies vanished, but their furniture endured. A few craftsmen continued to build it, refining and polishing the original designs. As this craft grew more sophisticated, stick furnituremaking became a recognized folk art. Recently, it has enjoyed a revival with the increasing interest in country and rustic furniture.

Among the best-known contemporary stick furnituremakers is Greg Adams of Muncie, Indiana, who made the swing shown. He is the proprietor of Willow, a shop in Muncie, but he's rarely there. He finds himself traveling a good deal, like his "gypsy" predecessors, demonstrating his craft. "It's a good trade to take on the road," he says. "You only need five tools — pruning shears, lopping shears, bow saw, hammer, and wire cutters. And you can find the materials almost everywhere."

He also explains that this sort of furnituremaking is unlike any other. "Most woodworking is very precise," Greg says. "This isn't. It's more forgiving, and there's more room for spontaneity and creativity."

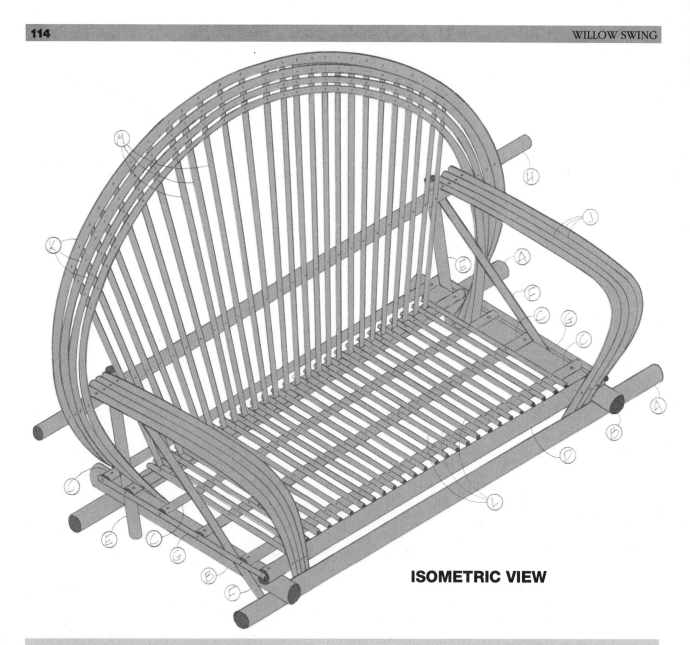

ISOMETRIC VIEW

Materials List

FINISHED DIMENSIONS

PARTS

A.	Swing rails (2)	2″ dia. x 52″
B.	Stretchers (2)	2″ dia. x 23¼″
C.	Seat rails (5)	1″ dia. x 41″
D.	Front seat rail	1½″ dia. x 41″
E.	Back supports (2)	1″ dia. x 18″
F.	Braces (2)	1″ dia. x 28½″
G.	End pieces (2)	½″ dia. x 18″
H.	Backrest	2″ dia. x 60″
J.	Arm boughs (8)	½″ dia. x 48″*
K.	Back loop boughs (4)	½″ dia. x 120″*
L.	Seat boughs (24–30)	½″ dia. x 18″*
M.	Back boughs (24–30)	½″ dia. x 38″*

Cut these parts to the lengths given, then trim them to their final length after you assemble the swing.

HARDWARE

10d Galvanized spiral decking nails (¼ lb.)

8d Galvanized spiral decking nails (¼ lb.)

6d Galvanized box nails (¼ lb.)

4d Galvanized box nails (¼ lb.)

1½″ Ring-shanked paneling nails (¼ lb.)

1″ Ring-shanked paneling nails (¼ lb.)

½″ Manila rope (40 ft.)

2″ Welded rings

Note: Before you begin, remember that all the dimensions in the Materials List and drawings are *approximate*. Because trees and saplings do not grow to precise dimensions, stick furniture does *not* require boughs of precise diameters or precise lengths. If you're overly concerned with precision, it may frustrate your attempt to build this project. In short: Loosen up and enjoy yourself.

1 Gather the willow.

According to Greg Adams, "Seventy-five percent of the skill needed to make a willow swing is in gathering the willow." You have to be part botanist, part outdoorsman, and part public relations specialist.

First of all, you have to know where willows grow. There are many different types of trees in the willow genus, but the most common are the black willow (in the East) and the goodding willow and arroyo willow (in the West). They all grow near water — you can find them in marshy areas, beside ponds, streams, and drainage ditches. Don't look for mature trees, but dense stands of small saplings that have grown for two to ten years. (See Figures 1 and 2.) These will be 4 to 16 feet tall, and reasonably straight.

Note: If willows are not common in your area, you can also use birch and elder saplings.

Once you locate a grove of young trees, ask the landowner for permission to harvest them. Most farmers consider willows to be a nuisance — the roots clog drainage ditches and streams. Most likely, they will gladly let you have all you want for free.

Cut the trees with a bow saw or lopping shears. Trim away the leaves and small branches so all you're left with are long, straight trunks and boughs. Group these into three piles — small (3/8″–3/4″ diameter), medium (3/4″–1/2″ diameter), and large (1 1/2″–2 1/2″ diameter). You'll need approximately 220 running feet of small willow, 30 running feet of medium, and 20 running feet of large. *Don't* cut the parts to size yet; the wood may dry before you can assemble it.

Warning: There are several hazards that you must avoid as you harvest the willow. In particular, watch out for ticks, snakes, groundhog holes, and bulls!

1/Willows tend to grow in dense groves near sources of water. Look for young, straight saplings, no more than ten years old.

2/You can identify the willows by their foliage. All the species in the genus have long, slender leaves. Most are pointed, such as these black willow leaves.

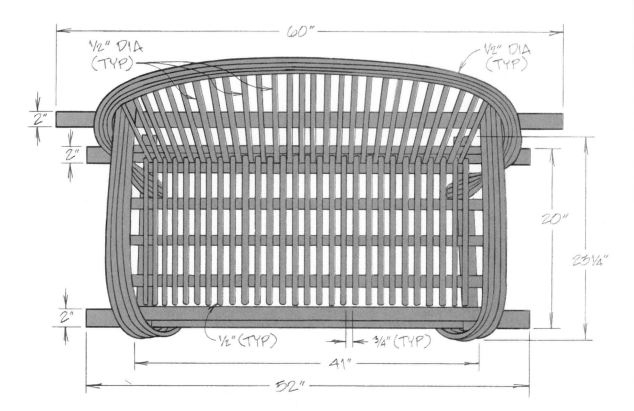

TOP VIEW

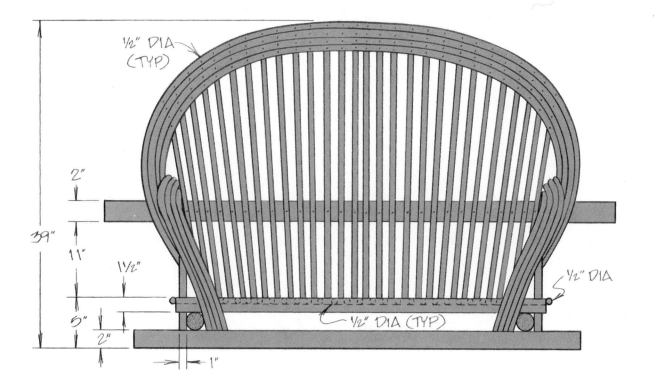

FRONT VIEW

2 **Gather the nails.** Stick furniture is assembled with small nails — simply drive a nail through one stick to fasten it to another. However, you need an assortment of nails, from 1″ long (2d) to 3″ long (10d). This will allow you to choose nails according to the diameters of the parts you want to fasten together. You want each nail to go *almost* all the way through both parts, without the point protruding.

Choose nails that are either galvanized or coated to prevent rust. Also, it's best to use nails with spiral or ring shanks, which keep them from working loose. (See Figure 3.) You won't be able to find spiral and ring-shanked nails in every size that you need, but spiral nails should be available in the larger sizes (8d and 10d), and ring-shanked in the smaller sizes (2d and 3d). If you can't find a spiral or ring-shanked nail in a certain size, buy ordinary box nails. (The shanks of box nails are slightly smaller in diameter than common nails — there's less chance the nail will split the wood.)

As you assemble the project, drive the nails so they will point either *down* or *back* in the completed swing, if possible. The sharp points should face away from you as you sit on the swing. If the point of a nail happens to come through the stock, snip it off with wire cutters.

Note: Even though the parts of this swing are fastened together with nails, none of the nails bears any weight. The weight of the swing (and the people sitting on it) is transferred directly from the seat to the swing

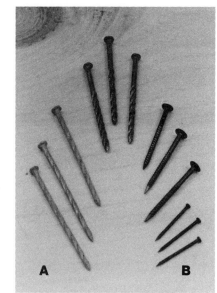

3/If you can, purchase spiral (A) and ring-shanked (B) nails to assemble the swings. The special shanks on these nails prevent them from working loose.

rails to the ropes. You needn't worry about the nails tearing loose — they only peg the parts together.

As you assemble the parts, you'll find the nails are relatively easy to pull out while the wood is still green. Once it dries, however, the wood shrinks around the nail shanks and they become much more tenacious. If you make a mistake during assembly, pull out the nails and correct it as soon as possible. The longer you wait, the more difficult it will become to disassemble the parts.

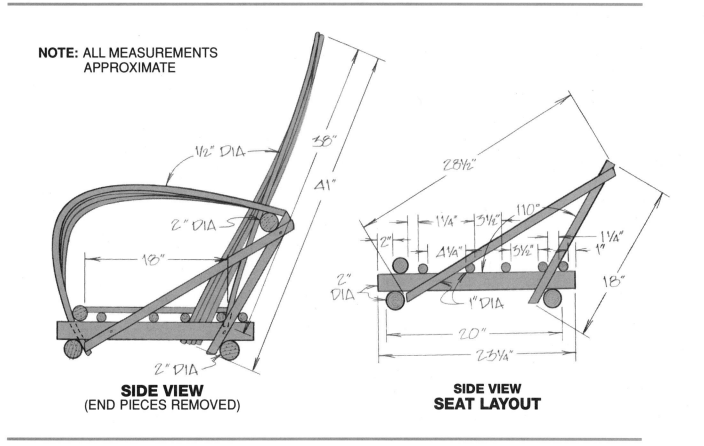

NOTE: ALL MEASUREMENTS APPROXIMATE

1/2″ DIA
38″
41″
2″ DIA
18″
2″ DIA

SIDE VIEW
(END PIECES REMOVED)

28½″
1¼″ 3½″ 110°
2″ 1¼″
4¼″ 3½″ 1″
2″ DIA
1″ DIA
18″
20″
23¼″

SIDE VIEW
SEAT LAYOUT

3

Assemble the swing rails and stretchers. Although the bent boughs and sticks make this swing look complex, it's actually very straightforward. The basic frame is just a simple trapezoid, slightly wider at the front than the back. Cut the swing rails and stretchers to the sizes specified in the Materials List, using a bow saw or lopping shears. Then nail the stretchers to the tops of the rails.

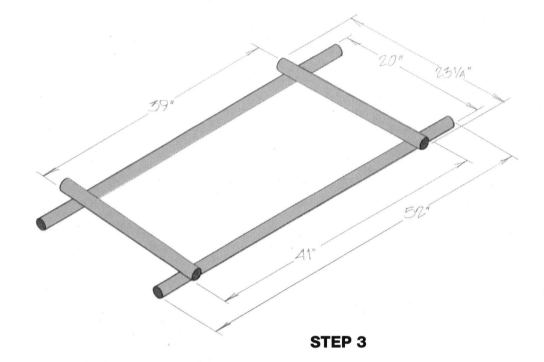

STEP 3

4

Attach the back supports and braces. Cut the back supports and braces to the sizes specified in the Materials List. Nail the back supports to the outside of the stretchers, just inside the back swing rails. Then attach the braces to the outside of the back supports and stretchers. As shown in the *Seat Layout/ Side View,* the braces hold the back supports 110° from the stretchers.

STEP 4

5

Attach the seat rails, backrest, and end pieces. Cut the seat rails and backrest to the sizes specified in the Materials List. Carefully select these rails — they should be as straight and as smooth as possible, so the seat will be fairly flat. The front seat rail should be about ½″ larger in diameter than the other five. This rail will become the front edge of the seat. If it's not large enough, the front ends of the seat boughs may poke the backs of sitters' legs.

Nail the seat rails to the tops of the stretchers. The two back seat rails flank the seat supports — one at the front, one at the back — to help hold them in position. When the rails are in place, attach the end pieces to the rail ends, and nail the backrest to the fronts of the seat supports.

Note: According to the designer, the end pieces serve no structural purpose, nor do they add much to the aesthetics. So why bother with them? "They'll hold a can or a glass while you're sitting in the swing," says Greg.

STEP 5

6

Attach and bend the arms. Cut the arm boughs to the size specified in the Materials List, using pruning shears. Nail one end of an arm bough to the backrest, just outside of a back support. Bend the bough in a graceful arch and nail the other end to the inside of the front swing rail. Repeat, nailing the next arm bough to the outside of the first one and bending it in exactly the same arch. Attach four boughs side by side to make each arm, and trim the ends flush.

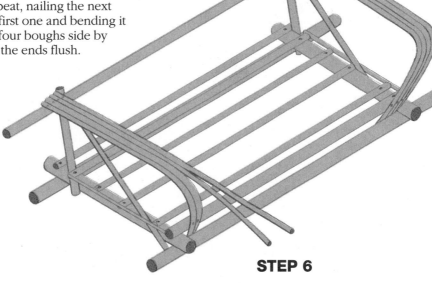

STEP 6

7

Attach and bend the back loops. Cut the back loop boughs to the size specified in the Materials List. Nail one end of a bough to the inside of a stretcher, just behind the third-from-the-back seat rail. Bend the bough around the arms and nail the other end to the other stretcher. Also, nail the bough to the front of the backrest where the parts cross. The bough should arch about 32″ above the back seat rail.

Repeat, nailing the ends of the next bough to the stretcher just behind the first bough. Bend this second bough so it arches slightly higher and wider than the first, but parallel to it as shown in the *Front View*. Nail it to the backrest just outside of the first bough. Repeat until you have attached four back loop boughs to the assembly. Trim the ends of the boughs flush.

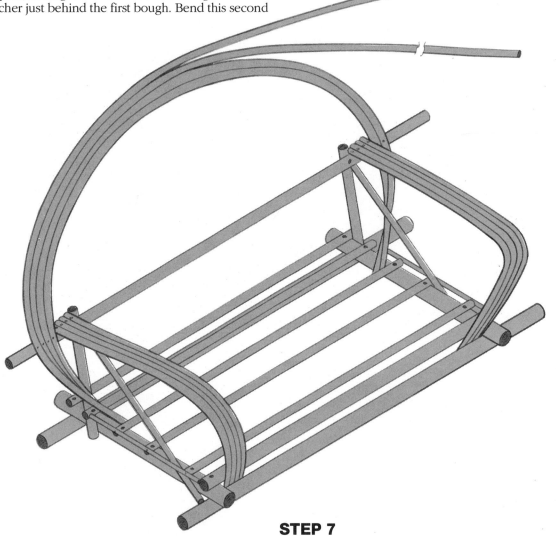

STEP 7

8

Attach the back and seat boughs. Cut the back and seat boughs to the sizes specified in the Materials List. Starting in the middle of the swing assembly, nail the bottom end of a back bough to the front of the back seat rail, and the top end to the back of the back loop. Trim the top end so it's flush with the outermost back loop bough.

Next, attach two seat boughs to the assembly, one on either side of the back bough. Nail the seat boughs to the top of the seat rails, positioning them so the back ends protrude about ½″ behind the back bough. Trim the front ends about ¼″ short of the front seat rail. (The tops of the seat boughs should be approximately flush with the top of the front seat rail.)

Attach two back boughs just outside the two seat boughs. Add two more seat boughs, then two more back boughs, and so on. Work from the middle of the swing toward the right and left sides until you have completely filled in the back and the seat.

TRY THIS! Back up these slender boughs with a *nailing anvil* as you drive the nails. This anvil is a small, dense piece of steel or iron that you hold in one hand while you hammer with the other. It keeps the parts from bending and flexing as you nail them together.

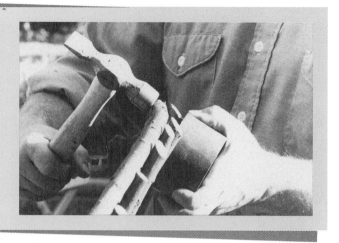

STEP 8

9 **Finish the swing.** Surprisingly, stick furniture will last almost as long as more sophisticated pieces if it's properly finished and cared for. Left untreated, the sticks will begin to split and the swing will fall apart in several years. (Greg finds that his untreated swings fall apart in 10–12 years.) But an exterior finish will prolong its life indefinitely.

Traditionally, stick furniture was finished with boiled linseed oil. This also stains the wood — the oil darkens as it ages, and turns the swing a deep brown in a few months. Unfortunately, linseed oil evaporates in time, and must be reapplied every year.

If you don't want to refinish the swing every year, you can also use clear exterior polyurethane, spar varnish, or a waterproof sealant. Wait several weeks to make sure the wood is dry, then apply several coats.

10 **Hang the swing.** To hang the swing, cut the Manila rope in six pieces — two 10' long, and four 5' long. Tie or braid one 10'-long piece and two 5'-long pieces to each welded ring, as shown in the *Hanger Rope Layout*. This will make two Y-shaped hangers, one for each side of the swing.

Tie the free ends of the 5'-long ropes to the swing rails, and the 10'-long ropes to the branch of a tree, porch rafter, or another suitable support for the swing. Loop the back 5'-long ropes behind the ends of the backrest. (See Figure 4.) Adjust the long ropes so the seat is about 18" off the ground, then adjust the short ones so the seat tilts back at 5° to 8°. Drive a nail through each short rope and into the rails to keep the rope from slipping.

4/To properly support the seat when you sit in the swing, you must loop the two short back ropes **behind** the backrest.

ATTACH TO SWING SUPPORT

10' APPROX

2" WELDED RING

5' APPROX

5' APPROX

ATTACH TO SWING

WHIP END TO PREVENT UNRAVELING

HANGER ROPE LAYOUT

Credits

About the Author: Nick Engler is a contributing editor to *American Woodworker* magazine, and teaches cabinet-making at the University of Cincinnati. He has written over 20 books on woodworking.

Contributing Craftsmen and Craftswomen:

Greg Adams (Willow Swing)

Bob Beason (Rocking Bench)

Larry Callahan (Victorian Porch Swing)

Nick Engler (Deacon's Bench, Folding Bench, Swing Frames, Lawn Glider)

Mary Jane Favorite (Adirondack Settee and Stool, Hobby Horse Glider, Child's Garden Bench)

Larry Heisey (Juggling Bench)

Gary Simon (Slab-End Bench)

Chris Walendzak (Garden Settle)

Note: Several of the projects in this book were built by woodworkers whose names have been erased by time. We regret that we cannot tell you who built them; we can only admire their craftsmanship. These include the Shaker Bench and Church Pew.

The designs for the projects in this book (that are attributed to a designer or builder) are the copyrighted property of the craftsmen and craftswomen who made them. Readers are encouraged to reproduce these copyrighted projects for their personal use or for gifts. However, reproduction for sale or profit is forbidden by law.

Special Thanks To:

Rich and Cheryl Critz

The Hen's Nest, West Milton, Ohio

Pat and Paul Hissong

Gordon Honeyman

Morning Sun Florist, Tipp City, Ohio

Mulberry Hill Collectibles, Inc., Tipp City, Ohio

Fred and Becky Sacks

Jacob Somerson

Bob and Jackie Wahl

Autumn Walendzak

Wertz Hardware Store, West Milton, Ohio

The Willow Tree Inn, Tipp City, Ohio

Rodale Press, Inc., publishes AMERICAN WOODWORKER™, the magazine for the serious woodworking hobbyist. For information on how to order your subscription, write to AMERICAN WOODWORKER™, Emmaus, PA 18098.

WOODWORKING GLOSSARY

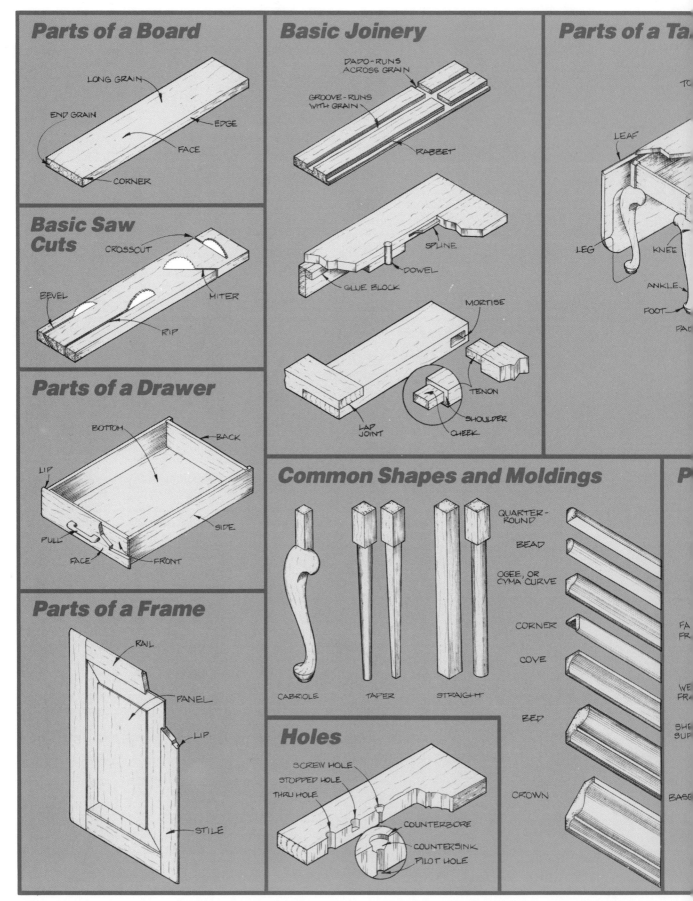

Parts of a Board

LONG GRAIN
END GRAIN
EDGE
FACE
CORNER

Basic Saw Cuts

CROSSCUT
BEVEL
MITER
RIP

Parts of a Drawer

BOTTOM
BACK
LIP
SIDE
PULL
FACE
FRONT

Parts of a Frame

RAIL
PANEL
LIP
STILE

Basic Joinery

DADO-RUNS ACROSS GRAIN
GROOVE-RUNS WITH GRAIN
RABBET
SPLINE
DOWEL
GLUE BLOCK
MORTISE
TENON
SHOULDER
CHEEK
LAP JOINT

Parts of a Ta...

TO...
LEAF
LEG
KNEE
ANKLE
FOOT
PA...

Common Shapes and Moldings

QUARTER-ROUND
BEAD
OGEE, OR CYMA CURVE
CORNER
COVE
BED
CROWN
CABRIOLE
TAPER
STRAIGHT

P...

FA...
FR...
WE...
FRA...
SHE...
SUP...
BASE...

Holes

SCREW HOLE
STOPPED HOLE
THRU HOLE
COUNTERBORE
COUNTERSINK
PILOT HOLE